Letters of a Mussoorie Merchant

Letters of a Mussoorie Merchant

Mauger Fitzhugh Monk

Introduction: **Ruskin Bond**

Edited by **Ganesh Saili**

NIYOGI
BOOKS

First published in 2006 by
Hugh Ashlet Rayner at the Pagoda Tree Press,
4 Malvern Buildings, Bath BA1 6JX

Complied & Edited by Andrew Morgan

Published by

NIYOGI BOOKS
D-78, Okhla Industrial Area, Phase-I
New Delhi-110 020, INDIA
Tel: 91-11-26816301, 49327000
Fax: 91-11-26810483, 26813830
email: niyogibooks@gmail.com
website: www.niyogibooks.com

Design: Shashi Bhushan/Niyogi Books

ISBN: 978-93-81523-07-0
Publication: 2012

Printed at: Niyogi Offset Pvt. Ltd., New Delhi, India

PUBLISHER'S NOTE

While going through these priceless letters describing the early years of Mussoorie and its inhabitants, we noticed something, which at the first glance, appeared like a mistake on the transcriber's part. Many words were given in a form that resembled modern-day texting rather than extracts from nineteenth century letters. This led to a lot reading up and research on the style of letter writing of the era. It was discovered that using wd, wh, and sufft as well as & for 'and', were all very common practice in handwritten English of this period (i.e. the 1830's -40's); especially when having to write letters for posting back to Britain, as postage rates were exorbitant, then (as now) and verbiage had to be kept to an absolutely bare minimum! Some letters were even written with two pages of text written on one sheet at 90° to each other, to save paper.

We decided to leave these abbreviations exactly as transcribed from the original manuscript letters to retain an authentic period feel, even at the risk of stretching the reader a little! We sincerely hope that we have done justice to the original character of the letters and their content. And the reader appreciates reading them as much as we enjoyed publishing them.

CONTENTS

FOREWORD

'No matter. Try again, Fail again, Fail Better.'
Samuel Beckett

Mauger Fitzhugh Monk was just the sort of person you would find in a Kipling story, had their paths ever crossed. In the late eighteenth and early nineteenth centuries many Europeans came to India in search of the pagoda tree, symbol of unlimited wealth and treasure. Some did indeed make their fortune; others ended up in the bazaars and byways of that 'great grey formless India' that so fascinated Rudyard Kipling.

However, Kipling came to Simla and Mussoorie many years after Mr. Monk had departed from this earth. Monk's tenure was brief. He arrived in Mussoorie in 1840 and left in 1849, dying in Meerut on his journey back to England and the Channel Islands.

Like the thousands who occupy the only land they still own when they die, Monk would have passed into oblivion but for the fact that his family preserved his letters and they have come down to us today in the form of this fascinating collection of correspondence, which reads like a novel—a story of strenuous endeavour met by total failure.

Yes, Monk was a failure. A failure at almost everything he attempted. And that is what makes him so fascinating. Because he could so easily have been you or me. If we survive, it is by dint of failing and trying again, and failing better!

Success stories are usually boring. The road to riches is usually built through the labours of those who are quickly discarded. You take someone's help and then bid goodbye to your helper. But

Monk wasn't smart enough to do that. He tried running a hotel, he tried running a school. He tried various things. But he was outsmarted by the big bosses, those who were already entrenched in the fledgling hill station; the likes of Mackinnon, who set up a brewery and made a fortune selling beer to parched British soldiers convalescing up at Landour.

Good old Mackinnon, he placated his conscience by helping to build a church a road and a school, and making sure that others did not compete with his establishments. The road, naturally, led to his breweries.

Monk's school survived somehow, in spite of the failure of his other business interests.

He married a pretty Eurasian girl, who gave him a son. But she died in childbirth a year or two later, and this left him rudderless again. His efforts to raise money became more and more pathetic. He married again—a mere child-wife. And finally he resolved to return to England to restore his fortunes. A fatal journey.

Why, then, are these letters so fascinating?

Chiefly because they throw light upon the social life of a hill-station in the early years of its development. At the time of Monk's arrival, Mussoorie was barely fifteen years old, the first residences having come up in the late 1820s. As far as I know, there is no other record or narrative of the hill-station's early years. And that is what makes it unique.

There were many in Mussoorie who were more successful than Monk, but they have not left us any accounts of their lives or the lives of those around them. Only the traveller, Fanny Parkes, has left us with a brief picture of Landour and Mussoorie in those very early days. The Mackinnons, the Youngs, the Wilsons were too busy being successful and left us no written legacy. It was more than a decade later that John Lang, the lawyer and newspaper proprietor put down his impression of the growing town, in his colourful and exaggerated prose. Because Monk's letters were private and not meant for publication, they give us an authentic picture of the town and its early days.

Lang was setting up his press in Meerut when our 'Mussoorie Merchant' was buried there. You won't find his grave in that vast city of the dead that occupies a corner of the old Meerut Cantonment; the inscriptions have worn away from most of the headstones. But in Landour's old cemetery you will find the grave of Elizabeth, his beloved wife. The tomb and inscription have stood the test of time. She rests in the shadow of tall deodars, facing the eternal snows.

Ruskin Bond
Landour, Mussoorie
15 July 2011

INTRODUCTION

The documents in this collection all relate to the life of Mauger Fitzhugh Monk, who was born in 1815 of an Irish father and a Guernsey mother. After schooling in Guernsey and apprenticeship in Plymouth, he qualified as a solicitor in 1836. But within a year he was serving in the East India Company Artillery under the assumed name of Gunner Fitzhugh O'Reilly. His three years in the ranks, his "restoration to respectability" as a schoolmaster, his agonised indecision whether to marry a beautiful girl of mixed race, the tragic course of their subsequent marriage, his disastrous business venture as hotelier and entrepreneur, his mysterious and sudden decision to return to England and his equally sudden death en route in 1849, form the substance of this volume. The story is bizarre enough, but piquancy is added by its being told, like an eighteenth century novel, in 'an epistolary style'.

The chief interest of these letters lies in Mauger's own character. Complex he certainly was. Dreamer, would-be scholar, entrepreneur, aspiring gentleman, recurrently reformed penitent, and near conman, he could play all these parts. Was he just a charming rogue? For sure, he had kissed the Blarney stone. He had the skills of a conman, but not the disposition. He could coin a good cliché, and could play the part of a ham actor when he thought, often wrongly, that the occasion demanded. But however distasteful to us his self-abasement before his father, and however self-deceiving his protestations of good intention, the man had 'Style'. This is evident even before Hannah Toussaint tells us so in the last letter of all. For Mauger may not quite have had panache or braggadocio, but breath-taking effrontery he did have. As a result, it is easy to overlook his enterprise and the range of his talents, and to ignore his diplomatic skills when being pressed by the parties in Guernsey to take sides in their quarrel. It is also easy to belittle his resilience. Mauger always bounces back. A man of more brittle temperament might have taken his brother William's path—suicide. But temperament apart, his greatest asset was a surprising one for a self-confessed moral coward. Despite catastrophic lapses, he did have reserves of moral courage, and on some critical occasions used them. For example, when he was at a low ebb in 1844, in broken health and facing ruin, he stood by his family and started again as a schoolmaster. A real cad would have disappeared. Or was this a case of Mauger pursuing, as always, the line of least resistance? The argument about him could be endless, but of one thing I am sure: I would not have bought anything, new or second hand, from him ... well, not more than once.

What does not appear in these letters? The biggest gap concerns the years 1837 to 1840, when Mauger was serving as Trooper Fitzhugh O'Reilly in the Artillery. We get a few glimpses [e.g. Nos. 26, 27 & 33] but that is all. And then there is 'the dog that did not bark', the subject that is just not mentioned, even though there is opportunity enough. Both Monks and Magraths had come from Ireland. Mauger's father was born and brought up there. Nicholas Magrath also. There were first cousins still living there, and Nicholas's own father and brothers were farming in County Longford. Letters in this collection make mention of the Potato Famine, both in Ireland and elsewhere, and of the suffering of the poor all over northern Europe; but no concern is expressed about the plight of their own kin. There is mention of cousins everywhere in the world but Ireland. Why the silence?

The social historian of the British in India could find much of interest here about the hill stations of Landour and Mussoorie in the 1840s, and about Rajpore, which lies at the foot of the hills on the road to Dehra. The odd shaft of light is thrown on the life of a Company's soldier at Dum Dum and Meerut, and there is a deal of reflected light from St. Peter's Port, Guernsey. A couple of glimpses of life in early New South Wales could be of interest to students of Australian history.

The letters themselves reached me in two batches, a few years apart. The first, known to be incomplete, came from my late cousin Una Monk who generously lent them to me. The missing second batch came to light later in the attic of another cousin, Dr. James Monk, who, like Una, was kindness itself in letting me have access to them. The reunited batches are now in the safe-keeping of Jim as head of the family. Most of the letters are written with the lines overlaid at right-angles, and on both sides of singularly thin paper. Luckily Mauger's expensive education had given him a clear hand.

This volume may never have seen the light of day without the support of Professor Alan Macfarlane. I owe him a very special debt of gratitude for his generosity.

Finally, I shall be glad to hear from any readers whose own interests and studies intersect with the matter of these letters.

Andrew Morgan
February 2006

WAYWARD YOUTH–DISASTER 1832-1840

LETTER I

From M. F. MONK, Mussoorie

To ISABELLA MONK, Guernsey.

[Endorsements:] Per Overland Mail.12 as.

14 JANUARY 1840

My Dearest Isabella,

You may perceive by the heading of my letter that I am now in a very different part of India from any I have hitherto visited & I trust on a journey, the object of which will shortly put an end to my mad military career. As I am well aware it will conduce to the happiness of all at home, more especially that of my dearest father to know that I am retracing the steps to, at least, respectability, I hasten to make you acquainted with my embryo prospects, sincerely hoping that my first steps from the ranks may meet the approval of those at home, whose approval I most value, as it has received the sanction of the only friends I can boast of in India, namely, that of the few officers who have been kind enough to evince any interest in me. To come to the point then, I am now on a month's trial touching my fitness & capacity to take the situation of Principal Classical Assistant in a school of great & increasing celebrity at a place called Mussoorie situate in the most healthy part of the lower range of Himalayas, & up to the present time have given every satisfaction.

I wish I could have delayed writing till the treaty had been definitely settled, but this is the last chance I have during the present month of writing by the overland mail for February. However in March or April's letter bag at farthest I shall send a full, true & particular account of situation, salary, in fact everything worth mentioning, & perhaps conclude with a list of school books & other necessaries, not procurable in either mountain or jungle, which I may stand in need of to teach the juvenile Anglo-Indian Idea[?] Latin & Greek—Memory of the marches of Hannibal, Alexander or Xenophon, what are we to the march of intellect? Fancy, dearest Bel, a classical vacation on the Himalayas, 7000 feet above the level of sea! My journey from Meerut here contained many of the usual adventures of Indian travelling, my palanquin broke down in the midst of a dense jungle & compelled me to walk nearly 30 miles till I could procure another—shortly after resuming my journey my bearers alarmed by the tracks of a tiger dropped me in the road & would have left me alone in my glory, but for the presence of a pair of most persuasive-looking pistols, objects in the hands of a Feringee[?] as alarming to any Hindoo as the sight of the Bengal bully himself. These and similar adventures diversified the monotony of being carried some three days in a box, the size of an extra-large coffin, till I reached the foot of the hills. To describe the ride up there is almost impossible: for to tell you the truth, mountain travelling here is of so peculiar a character, such exquisitely nervous work, that it would do no more than depict sensations—how I felt, as mounted on an obstinate, wilful, cat-quality-possessing pony, yclept in these regions, a Ghoont, I found myself at one moment, at the discretion of the tiny-mountain-monster, escalading the face of a mountain at the imminent hazard of slipping over the wretch's rump: at another, descending in a crab-like fashion a precipitous ravine or if the road were somewhat level, calculating the precise height of a gorge, some 300 feet in depth, along the very outermost edge of which, (& only on the outermost edge will the stubborn but sure-footed Ghoont walk) my self-willed Bucephalus, about three feet & a half high, was bearing his quaking burthen, who, with clenched teeth & suppressed aspiration was quietly resigning himself to what appeared his inevitable fate.

I certainly was disappointed in finding the Himalayas so totally different from what my imagination had pictured them, no fertile valleys, no roaring torrents, but mountain after mountain rising abruptly one after the other, their bases masked by gullies formed by mountain streams during the monsoons, & even these are for the most part covered with a brushwood impervious to the eye. Mussoorie is built on various eminences, the bungalows perched wherever nature has pointed out a favourable spot but for the most part at the distance of many hundred yards from each other. The school occupies a ridge the adjacent ravines of which have been filled in or built over, & incredible labour has been bestowed upon the formation of even a playground. Tho' not established more than five years, the establishment boasts of nearly one hundred boarders of the best families in northern India to many of whom a sufficient education is here afforded, the plains of Indostan being the field of their future fortunes, whilst to many more it serves but as a preparation for the higher schools of India [&] England. Mussoorie enjoys a similar climate to that of the more northern parts of England at least, so say the old residents, & I believe them, for after two years in the plains, I find hard frosty mornings such as we have now rather too cool to be pleasant. It is considered, however, the healthiest spot in Bengal, & is not quite 2 miles from the Grand Convalescent Depot of that Presidency.

More on this subject I have not now to say & now, my dearest sister, let me request that your future letters, & I trust I may receive many from you, may not be composed as most of the letters I have received from home have hitherto been, almost entirely of sermons or reproaches. Magrath & Uncle William are the only two of my correspondents, who have appeared to think that making them the principal subject of an epistle was quite unnecessary. If my present experience, past suffering & common sense are insufficient to make me a better man, sermons never will;- as for reproaches, there is but one person from whom I am prepared to bear them: he has abstained from them, let no one else then throw the stone when he has stayed his hand. A few weeks more will, I trust, emancipate me from the H.C.'s livery; the seal that bound me not to address my father in writing, whilst I remained a soldier, will be broken & I can then ask forgiveness under my own hand for the errors of which I have been guilty.

You may now expect to hear from me monthly by the overland—for charity's sake let me hear often from home. I only received three letters from Europe during the whole of last year —one from you & two from Clapton. I wrote in May, June, July & October; let me know in your next if any of those letters have been received. Time passes, I must [... ...] say adieu. With kindest love to my dear father, brothers, sisters, nephews, nieces, &c &c, & best regards to all enquiring friends, I remain my dearest Bell,

Your ever affectionate brother,
M. F. Monk.

P.S. Direct to Mr. Monk, Mussoorie Seminary, Upper Province, Bengal.

LETTER II

From Col. W. S. WHISH, Dum Dum

To HUGH MONK, Guernsey

[Endorsements:] "Per Steamer. H. Monk Esq. Ann's Place, Guernsey, via Bombay Alexandria & England." "14 March 1840" "8 May 1840"

12 MARCH 1840

Dear Sir,

I had the pleasure of receiving your letter of 20 November, on the 27th ulto, and had scarcely perused it, or had time to conjecture whether your kind arrangement for your son, would prove acceptable to him when a letter from him, of the 16th ulto was put into my hands, urging me to procure his discharge and shewing good cause for the same. The next morning I waited upon the Commander-in-Chief, to solicit sanction, which, having obtained, (after brief explanation of the circumstances), I without delay authorised the necessary course to be adopted, and as I cannot without losing the present mail (which will be despatched on the 16th inst.) defer writing to you till the arrangements for your son's manumission have been virtually completed; I give you a few lines by the earliest opportunity that you may be the sooner freed from all misgivings on that score and I wrote to him on the 29th ulto. He has entered into an engagement with Mr. Mackinnon (a worthy man, be it noted, who was also a Private in the regiment a very few years ago) to undertake for two years, the duties of

Principal Classical Assistant at the seminary at Mussoorie on the monthly salary of 150 Rps for the first year and of 200 Rps for the second year, with quarters, the particulars of which he will no doubt duly communicate to you. When I hear from him again, I shall be better able to judge the propriety or necessity of his availing himself of your present liberality, or of any part of it. In making application for his discharge to government I had only to say that the sum of 400 Rps was forthcoming and if he remit that sum to me, (as I think, he will prefer doing) I shall destroy the Letters of Credit on Cockerell & Co.

You will no doubt communicate this agreeable intelligence to Mrs. Foot & I beg you will say, with my kind regards, that I am exceedingly obliged to her, for having made me instrumental to the furtherance of an object, she (and you), had so much at heart, and which under the blessing of God will restore your son to a sphere of duty more congenial, to his taste and acquirements, and where his talents with habits of industry and steadiness cannot fail to bring him into any favourable notice. I am, Dear Sir,

Your faithful & obedient servant,
W. S. Whish.

LETTER III

From M. FitzH. MONK, Mussoorie, Lower Range, Himalaya
To HUGH MONK, Guernsey.

13 APRIL 1840

My Dearest Father,

Once more after a lapse of now nearly three years, do I again venture to address you but to announce that which, I feel, cannot but give you the highest satisfaction &, I trust, serve as a balm to the wound occasioned by the contents of the last communication I penned to you in England. The step which I took to relieve myself of temptations and companions from whom I had not strength of mind at once to sever myself & remain in Europe has, & will doubtless still be of advantage to me. The strictness of military discipline compelled me to adopt strict habits of regularity, an unwillingness to become the boon companion of the persons about me, induced sobriety, & I believe, a natural desire to show myself mentally superior to my comrades & to obtain employment kept me from the various excesses & derelictions of duty, to which, either from impulse or inclination, I might have been tempted. I trust I have left the army a better man than I entered it. Physically I am no worse & am stouter & bigger than I ever was before. Col. Whish informs me in a letter date of the 29th Feb last that the day your letter reached him, he also received one from me, requesting the exertion of his interest towards procuring my discharge, the money for which had been lodged at the Division Office at

Meerut. He at the same time, promised to use his influence, & my discharge from the H.C.'s service has been signed, but the document, has not yet reached me. Having, however, received official intimation of its being granted, I hasten to announce my freedom to you, & trust my aunt's letter may have prepared you for the news. Let me also add my unfeigned gratitude for your kindness & liberality in seconding my views and the assistance so readily tendered to aid my exertions in regaining a station in society but undeserving as I am of such goodness, I should be still more so, were I under the circumstances in which I am placed, to avail myself of the aid, you must have deprived yourself of many, very many needful comforts to bestow. Accept then, my dearest father, my sincerely offered thanks & comfort yourself with the assurance of your son's regeneration, & that his first step is but the earnest of his future exertions. I need scarcely add that I have desired Col. Whish to return your bounty. I have entered into an engagement with the master of a school of growing celebrity as principal assistant for two years, the first at a salary of 150 Rps, the second at that of 200 per month, but would not undertake for the higher branches of mathematics or I could have obtained a better salary. There are four [?] subordinate ushers, so I meddle not with the boys out of school—my duty being the instruction of the upper classes in Latin, reading, writing & arithmetic. If any boys wish it, I am also to teach drawing. In addition to my salary I have apartments, medical attendance & fuel. This I think you will not pronounce bad for the first step.

The climate of Mussoorie is considered the most salubrious in India & of its good effects I can offer a practical illustration in my own person having grown excessively stout during the few weeks I have been here. Among the numerous productions of the soil, I recognise very many plants, the names of which you used to tell us in our afternoon rambles in that dear little island, which I fear it will be many years ere I can again revisit. What would I not give to be amongst you even for a week!

In what direction I shall next bend my views I have not yet made up my mind but by steady application to the native Persian languages as well as to mathematics, shall endeavour to fit myself for any situation that may come within my reach or the scope of my interest. At teaching I mean to remain no longer than suits me, after my engagement is fulfilled. And now, my dear father, I am going to turn beggar, but with one exception, I do not think you will deem my petition unreasonable. The exception is a watch, one not for ornament merely but a watch that will keep time, for I have not given up all idea of the "Trigonom: Survey"; deeming a good government situation superior to any other, & in taking observations, even for common domestic & general purposes one that will keep time is here invaluable. The other things I have to ask are classical books, principally Latin, if they can be spared, viz. Livy & Tacitus; Ellis's Exercises, Edward's Grammar, Horace, Virgil, & a Dictionary & Gradus. (Cicero & Sallust I have been able to purchase) to which be pleased to add a Lexicon Gr: Testament Analecta Minora, (the Majora I have) & Herodotus. These with a box of colours in good order, a case of Matheml-Instr, & such really good mathematical works as you can spare me to be packed in boxes, not exceeding 30 lbs weight each, will be of essential service to me. I have tried two or three Matheml-Instr cases, which are sold here most extravagantly but they are all Brummagem, warped & with Tangent scales invariably falsely marked. The Government ones are 120 Rupees a set, & not to be procured except thro' an officer of the survey. I should also like to have the "Lyons Medal" & any good books you may wish to send me, for my evenings are as solitary as a hermit's.

I trust my request may not be deemed unreasonable, for books are not procurable in the Himalayas, but wives sometimes are, so let me seriously ask your consent & permission to take unto myself a better half should I light upon a lady upon whom I can conscientiously throw myself away, as soon as I deem myself capable of maintaining her. If a tone of levity should appear to you to pervade this letter pray excuse it: for since the news of my release reached me I have been "un peu fou" & from want of practice have made many interlineations which I know you do not like. Pardon them all, & if the prospect of your prodigal son's becoming an useful member of society brings one cheering ray to the heart of my poor dear father, let me know it under his own hand; for your first letter will bring greater happiness to me than a reprieve to a condemned criminal. I have written to Wm. with all love to my dear brothers & sisters, but I trust my dearest sister Isabella will become a regular correspondent. God bless you, my dear father, may you live long & be happy. This shall be the nightly prayer of your fast amending & I trust

Ever affectionate son,
M. Fitzh Monk.

P.S. Direct the boxes to Mr. Monk, at Mr. Mackinnon's, Mussoorie, Bengal, care of P. O'Brien Esq., Calcutta. The letters the same. I write per Overland Mail: but no "O'Brien" on the letters which by the Overland route will reach me in less than 3 months, decidedly the safest way, as well as the quickest.

LETTER IV

From MAUGER MONK, Mussoorie
To ISABELLA MONK, Guernsey.

6 JUNE 1840

My Dear Bell,

Those dear four letters of your familiar Christian name, but remind me more forcibly of its concomitant surname; with what pleasure have I resumed it! How glibly does my pen run as I sign the monosyllable—sworn never to be resumed till I have worked out my deliverance from the bondage to which I had voluntarily sold myself and for what? The honour of being shot at for the nominal sum of 1/4′ per diem. I call it nominal, for trifling as it is the Hon. Company by valuing the rupee at 2/6 have robbed the unfortunate soldier of 1/5 of his stipulated pay and they that have done this deed are "honourable men". A few days more and the arrival of my discharge will make me clear of them. My money has been lodged these three months, but my manumittance has not yet come. Press of military business consequent on the war in Afghanistan and the declaration of hostilities against China has probably caused the delay; but even with the Commander-in-Chief's gracious letter allowing me "the liberty of purchasing my discharge" I feel anxious to learn that Gunner F. O'Reilly is no longer one of the H.C.'s fighting men. I leave the name without the slightest mark against it, and had when I left Meerut for the hills the favourable & volunteered testimony of four officers, under whom I had served, as to my sobriety, intelligence, attention, and soldierlike conduct and appearance. A little of the mammon[?] of dress, you see, left—in fact I was particular about the make of my clothes; they were, though I say it who should not, as poor Young used to remark, the best cut in the company:- my boots, gloves and forage cap of course faultless. A propos des bottes these articles are made in the most excellent style by the native cordwainers of good material and inferior only in their workmanship to London boots at the small charge of from one to two rupees. I have often seen them sold for less than the first-named price. Two pairs last me the year well. A decent forage cap, could not be had for less than 6 rupees = 15 shillings but with care would last 3 or 4 years. So much for military clothing but I cannot quit the subject without adding that our uniform was uglier & the materials infinitely worse than that of the Guernsey Militia Artillery. But to what think you I am indebted for my present situation. Though I have been Pay & Provost Sergeant, tutor to officers' children, personal defence[?] to poor devils tried by courts martial; petition scribbler in chief, parson's clerk, and sermon reader on the line of march, president & secretary of the Temperance Society, in short in continual employ, and to none of these can I trace my introduction to notice. To the Meerut Artillery Theatricals and my attendance on public auctions to purchase Hindustani and Persian works do I owe my rise. An imaginary view of the Bolan Pass at the time this army was on the march to Caubul, with the artillery attacked in one of the most desperate gorges; and subsequently a series of tableaux vivants representing the capture of Ghuznee, with appropriate scenery, procured me even editorial notice. My works were thought worthy of criticism and the Bolan Pass, (the drop scene) pronounced vigorous & artistical. My performance of Capt. Stevens in the farce of that name was stated to be "gentlemanly", my Latin quotations in 'Dr. Pangloss' "evidently understood by the actor" but Monsr.

Morbleu in *Monsr Tonson* put the climax on the whole. The French accent was declared perfect; no Cockney "ong's" & "ing's", and "the correct pronunciation of the critical 'u' and the guttural 'r'", declared by a Gallo-Greek merchant to be "inconcevablement bien pour un Irlandois" as my name proposed.

Now my dear girl, dont set this down to vanity, it is a plain fact, and though I should be loth to tell lies to others I have not scrupled to be thus egotistical in a portion of my letter to you. To show you at the same time how much I am indebted to chance, whilst you may draw your own conclusions as to the morality of our amusements in this enervating clime. The least exertion during the greater portion of the year is necessarily accompanied by great exhaustion, which however produced in turn its own remedy—sleep; here indeed "tired natures sweet restorer, healing sleep". For I have invariably rose from a rest of this nature more refreshed and without that depression of spirits, the eternal companion of the indolent habits unfortunately adopted by many Europeans during the hot season, than if I had succumbed to the weather and used the stimulants too frequently had recourse to by those around me. Since I came to India I have used the daily allowance made by the H.C. and never indulged; now a bottle of brandy lasts me a month, or in the shooting season I may use two. If there is a man who has imbibed a strong liking for ardent spirits let him learn but once of the two lessons I have learned. Let him be sent to wait on a comrade in the horrors as they are here too truly named & he must be a wretch devoid of feeling, if ever he forget. To two such scenes has duty led me, to be a witness, in one a fine muscular handsome young Irishman perished from the effect of intemperance, not habitual; for some hours a glowering maniac, whom it was my duty to watch the livelong night & prevent his committing suicide. I thought the night would never end. It did at last, but death came in the morning. Think you I could ever forget that scene. Never while memory holds him dear. Good night, dear Bell, I shall continue my epistle to-morrow.

Now to recommence but where in the world, on sea or land is the letter Aunt in her dear kind epistle of 12th Decr last mentions as being then in the act of being written by you? Sarah alludes to it in February's letter as supposed to contain all local news? I have set my heart upon receiving it & shall be greatly disappointed if it reach me not. Did you send it by post? Or is it coming by ship? I trust it is not lost, but fear it may have shared the fate of not a few of my own scrawls wh I have every reason to believe could never have reached England or the constant charge of not writing often enough would never have been so constantly repeated. It is my intention to write to some one member or other of the family every overland mail, that is monthly, but must not, I find delay doing so to the eleventh hour, for our post office is near seven miles from here, & some eleven or twelve hundred feet higher than we are, & the authorities not overparticular in giving regular notice of the latest day on wh letters can be received by them. It is moreover no uncommon thing to see a notice in the paper announcing the loss of particular mails, the dak-hurkaries being murdered on the road or carried off by tigers, & the letter bags stolen or their contents set adrift at the mercy of the four winds of heaven. Since arriving here I have written to dear Aunt Wm (Letter sent 12th March) and to my dear father [31 above] & Wm. on the 13th April. May's mail I was too late for, but I am now trying to make up for it in June & in addition to this intend writing to Sarah & Magrath (a joint letter). I wish my dear sister Margaret wd make me acquainted with her handwriting & style of correspondence. A line or two just notices her state of health & where she is or if she has been unwell, but no other news of her whatever. Give her a most loving kiss from me & tell her that I shall most seriously, most funnily or most amusingly answer any communication she may honour me with, according to her own directions. I shd think she must be familiar with all the scan. mag[sic] of the day—young ladies of her age at least are generally so in spite of the authoress of the Life of Cromwell's system of education. I hope your worthy governess Mrs. Sargent is well & that my fair & fat sister Madge has benefited by her tuition.

My memory is so bad that I scarce recollect the contents of a letter I have written a month after; but I sincerely hope my first epistle from India to my poor dear father gave him some little happiness & pleasure. I scarcely knew how to address him, in fact, I did not know how, so penned according to the impulse of the moment. I tried to qualify my return of assistance I had asked of him before by requesting something else, more as a token of his forgiveness, than for any other object. I have since thought it may look like selfishness but do not think my motive such. I have been so often taxed with it in letters from Europe that I have grown quite sensitive on that score. It has become a complete thorn in my side. I have asked for some books to be sent me, as necessary, to my present situation, I shall in all probability request more, shd the Pedagogue's duties suit my views, but until I learn from home that I shall be allowed to pay for anything purchased on my account, I shall most decidedly not trouble you to send me any things but those that are disposable from home. There are some of my old acquaintances, such as, my desk, portfolio & medal I shd be glad to see again but except in the event of my sending a very large order, do not let any parcels exceed 30 lbs weight & as each having to be carried for six week's journey on a human being's head, will cost me £2.10 for carriage; from England here, let them be as near that weight as possible. A large package, tho' not proportionably expensive, will be two months longer reaching me.

I have much that I could say & inquiries I wish yet feel ashamed to make. A few months more will put it in my power to cancel many of the pecuniary obligations, under wh I laboured on quitting England but this is man's business, not ladies so I shall drop the subject with you & reserve it for Magrath. I wd fain recover my good name at home as well as my station here. Presuming that the contents of my letters to Ann's Place, the Pollet & Clapton become mutually known I shall endeavour to vary them as much as possible so as not to tire you with a constant repetition. Further I have no wish that their contents, in detail, shd go but dear Aunt Mauger [Clapton] has been I may say a second mother to us all, & I know feels an interest in the welfare of her protegés, however unworthy, one at least, has shown himself of her kindness. But he is changed I trust for the better. Magrath is a prince of a fellow, so you may in future take whatever is written to them as intended to reach home.

I little suspected when the Wellesley lay a few miles below Calcutta in March last, poor Henry might be on board. Heaven prosper him now he is started in the world. I have just written him a letter of advice, wh I trust may find him. Adml Maitland is dead & the squadron under Rear Admiral Elliot of Chinese notoriety. Remember me kindly to the old servants particularly my good old nurse Mary—Mrs. Lakeman, I beg pardon. I trust she thrives on matrimony & John Wesley. Give all sort of kisses to Margaret & Sarah's bairns, Papa's pet, Little Hugh, Miss Ellen & young-to-me-nameless. Don't forget my message to the first. All brotherly affection to Dr. W. P. [William]. Love to Uncles & Aunt Wm & send them my letter for perusal. The recollection of my residence with them whilst in town is the only one that brings with it any pleasure. (Dear Aunt, Bless you & uncle for yr many kindnesses & give my best regards to Mrs. Cowan & Robert.) My poor dear father has too much cause to have me ever in his remembrance. My most filial love to him, for whose restoration to health & happiness I daily pray & whose blessing & forgiveness I wd fain obtain. To Glatney & Clifton my sincere regards, & kind remembrances to all inquiring friends & rival doctors & believe me ever to be,

Your most devotedly attached brother,
M. Fitzh Monk.

P.S. I trust my dear father has had no return of his attack in the eyes, & hope my letter to him may have proved a salve. With aunt & uncle you must have had a pleasant trip to the lakes & suppose your letter (coming) contains a full true & particular acct thereof. I await its arrival with impatience. I shall be glad at any time to get any useful letters of introduction & mind to give me notice overland of parcels coming out, their number & the name of the ship that [stops there].

LETTER V

From MAUGER MONK, Seminary, Mussoorie
To NICHOLAS MAGRATH Esq, Surgeon R.N., Pollet St.,
Guernsey, Channel Isles. 'Per Overland Mail'.
Endorsed: 'Landour. 1840 June 5 [sic] Paid 12 Annas.'

8 JUNE 1840

My Dearest Sister & ever esteemed Nicholas,

I do not mean to let this overland mail escape me without answering yr most welcome letter, tho' I shd have liked Magrath's postscript all the better for being a little longer—better however what there is than none at all. It reached me the 25th ulto & little did either of you suspect that at the time you were writing I was on a month's trial for the situation I at present hold, "Head Assistant of Mussoorie Seminary". To the astonishment of diverse country born scholars, who had written most flowery un-English letters of application a b----y[sic] soldier was preferred before them & that without any examination. Mackinnon, who has established the school, is making money fast, & is, as far as I am enabled to judge, a tolerably liberal Scot. His attempts at first were looked upon as the efforts of a visionary, but he has persevered & succeeded & talks of returning to Scotland in five years or more to settle & superintend the education of his young family. He has a strong turn for mechanics & hopes that his sons, the youngest of who is but just breeched, may also have an inclination that way. Altogether he has now five children living, with a strong probability of an increase, wh may perhaps change his views but shd it not, at the end of a term of apprenticeship, there may be an opening for your humble servant. He is an able mathematician & a man of good general information but not, I think, my superior in the classics. I am endeavouring to make up my deficiency but Euclid & I do not agree. I have become by practice an excellent arithmetician, but can make but little headway either in the mathematics or the native languages;- on the latter I must be in a furious passion ere I can pronounce my words distinctly & without a French accent, which I invariably use to the great detriment of the language & the amusement of bystanding Englishmen, when I am quietly addressing a native. Time & perseverance will get me over this vile habit: at present, I am compelled to get the steam up before I venture to give a long order to my servants.

Mackinnon, like most of us, has his faults certainly not amiable ones. He is self-willed, obstinate & passionate. Any suggested alterations in the established system throw him into a perfect fury, wh terminates in the sulks, & the alteration in his manner to you is visible to all the scholars. I had a row with him on this subject originating I believe in the quantity of a word:- requested an explanation of him & desired for the future any misunderstanding might not become a subject of discussion amongst the boys, shook hands, and now we understand each other & are better friends than ever. To avoid future controversy, I have however laid it down as a rule to pursue his own system of education, & do neither more nor less than my prescribed duty. He can't throw the uniform in my face, for he too was an artilleryman & often tells the boys that Mr. Monk & himself were Essedaric, barring the difference of the scythes on the axles, wh we, more polished warriors than Caesar's brave opponents, did not deign to use. Polished doubtless we were more than they. Helmets they disdained & I don't think sported black "tigers" for the daily burnishing their arms and accoutrements. Their want of polish was made up of valour, the better part of wh, I humbly opine, to be discretion.

Let me now try to vary the subject. I have written a long letter to Bell, even more egotistical & full of personalities than this—for personalities, read, self—but I did not at first like to write it but what can you expect from a poor devil, who has three classes under his care to instruct daily in Latin, History, Arithmetic & writing, who is immured with them for six hours for five days in the week, & on the sixth for two; whose peregrinations consist in riding to church on Sunday 3 miles up hill & more, & the same distance down again; in a quiet stroll on pony-back after five o'clock in the evening for the benefit of musing & fresh air, or a ramble down some two or three hundred feet, gun in hand, into the extremely narrow ravines, which skirt the bases of the mountains, in search of a hill partridge or a couple of brace of green pigeons, or of the many variety of dove to be found here; mayhap, occasionally, lighting on a pheasant or a deer, but at the risk of a personal encounter with a bear or a leopard shd you stray too far from human habitations; almost certain of seeing the disgusting hyena, never here known to face man, even when wounded, tho' possessing by far the most powerful jaws of any known animal. These rambles are not frequent—the return requires too great an exertion of the lungs, & promotes too copious a perspiration to make their repetition pleasant—besides the evenings are too short to admit of great slaughter in the green wood, so I cannot boast of my success as a sportsman; once I killed a bear, whose skin formed a mat for some time, but it harboured fleas so I discarded it. But this, I mentioned in my letter to Wm, wh I suppose you have seen. What can you expect from one whose leisure hours are for the most part devoted to study? From one whose almost only companionable associates are his thoughts & his cheroot? For I cannot call the recently emancipated school-boy louts of ushers, companions, whose conversations savour of nothing but rice & curry; who stare with astonishment at a straight forward proposition, as tho' there lurked therein some to them infathomable plot, & who to save their lives could not give a direct & unhesitating answer to a plain but perhaps abruptly put question. Pshaw! It is almost a taste to exchange with them the common courtesies of life. The country-born & the half-caste for the most part (for I have met a few, a very few exceptions) combine the worst failings of the European & the native without any of their redeeming qualities. With assistance & contributions from home (for books are not procurable here) I trust to be enabled to form a small but select & companionable library, & when I can furnish a house & maintain a wife to look out for a better half. I have a sort of presentiment the hills will be my home for some time to come & as they are deemed the healthiest part of Northern India, I might have a worse place of residence.

And now I want you to let me know what debts of mine, if any, remain unpaid, & claims for which have been sent in. On this subject even at this distance from home, I feel an indescribable antipathy to addressing my dear father personally. That I am ashamed of myself is not sufficient to express my sensations; they are a compound of anxiety not to hurt his feelings or rake up the dregs of the bitter draught I have made him swallow, of shame at my own misconduct & fear of I know not what. The subject is one wh hangs like a cloud over me, & the knowledge of my errors checks that fearlessness of thought & action wh ought to be innate in every man of principle. Let me know in your next if Whiteford, Little & Foot have been paid—in fine, how my affairs stand, for altho' for the first twelve months I shall be unable to advance anything, I trust in the succeeding ones to save sufficient to save my name from disgrace by paying everyone his due. As you are housekeepers I will enter into a detail of my mode of living & expenses. My monthly salary is equivalent to £15, five of wh I pay to Mr. Mackinnon in part liquidation of £60 I borrowed of him to purchase my discharge & an outfit. The first cost £40. Out of the remaining £10, my messing amounts to £5-10, servants £2-10, Moonshee or native teacher £1, & keep of horse 10/s. Ten shillings serves me for pocket money & the remaining £2 is paid to the native merchants who supplied me with crockery, cooking utensils &c &c, all wh I had to purchase together with a little furniture, for my rooms had only the bare walls when I entered them. A few months more & I shall be very comfortable but you may see that I cannot save for the first year, everything in this fashionable invalid station being twice as dear as in the plains, owing in some measure to the greater expense of carriage up the hills, everything from a pin to a cannon being carried by men.

Aunt in her answer to one of my rather short letters expressed a wonder that I did not write more, living in a land teeming with objects of interest as I do. Interest indeed! Yes there is enough of both principal & interest in the mercantile race of this country:- self interest there is indeed plenty of: in the half-caste, country-born & native communities self interest & the interest on money are the only subjects in wh they take any interest; of the Europeans I know only the race, who dwell in barracks: with them interest was 4 annas in the rupee per mensem, exactly six hundred per cent. On the only two occasions that I visited Calcutta, a piece of American drill, a few books & a bottle or two of soda water were the only interesting things I saw & purchased, for the air was like a furnace seven times heated & when you are faint from heat & a seven miles ride in such an atmosphere I never mentioned what can you take an interest in, save a cool room & cooling drinks. At Benares the once splendid capital of Bengal & still abounding in beautiful buildings I was detained four hours at the pay-office with two drunken prisoners & upwards of 3000 Rupees in my charge (for when I passed thro' I was Pay Sergt Provost Sergt Adjutt's & Detachment writer) with a sepoy guard under my command, the treasure sentries of wh would salute me every time I passed in spite of my orders to the contrary, for I was subject to a court-martial both for allowing them aye even for returning their greeting. This added to the trouble I was put to by finding half the detachment drunk as owls on my return left me no time to inspect the far famed Hindoo holy of holies. In the winter vacations (the only one we have in the year) I shall perhaps visit Delhi or Agra both however I mean to see some time or other & give you accounts of them but next spring D.V. I shall certainly go & see the greatest fair in the world at Hurdwar, only three days' ride from here. To a soldier India teems with petty & unavoidables[sic] annoyances, wh however little in themselves are enough on the Scotch principle that every Mickle macks a muckle to form a sum total that wd spoil the sweetest temper in the world, to wit musquitoes, flies, creeping & flying bugs in swarms, raving drunkards at night, cockroaches, tarantulas, centipedes, the danger arising from asps & snakes, oppressive & enervating heats, bad liquor, the insolence of natives, who sneer at & rob you at the same time, not to mention, vexatious drills, harassing & useless marches, & last but not least in my catalogue, dismally lonely posts, when the yelling of a jackal & the unearthly laugh of the hyena keep up a fearful accompaniment to reflections forced at that most unseasonable hour upon one by an upbraiding conscience or the uninvited reminiscence of past misconduct.

But I must bring this to a conclusion without commenting on the Guernsey news, as I had intended; but tell me, who in the world did Captn Henvey bestow himself upon? A viscountess in her own right surely? For I saw in the *Spectator* that they had perpetrated a child betwn them, & had never heard of the marriage. Give my kindest love to Aunt Eliza & Uncle Joseph, to the former I wd like to write, but a "letter of condolence" wh it must be, is beyond my ability. Tell me in your next how you think she wd receive one from me. I know for some years I have been no favourite. Don't forget poor Uncle Davey & by all means let the dear, kind, folks at my Clapton "home" have my letter, tho' by no means an interesting one, & tell Bell to send hers too. I wd not for worlds omit ought that may interest the kindest of women. Send me Cousin Lambe's address and let any one writing to Clifton fail not to communicate all kindest regards to himself, Mrs. L & family with my best respects & most grateful thanks to Mrs. Foote for her kind introduction to Col. Whish. I am happy that Henry is in the R.N. & am endeavouring to ascertain his locality to write him. My dear father's health & happiness is now the subject of my daily prayer. Kiss your dear chicks for their Uncle Mauger, whom you may one day point out as an example & warning. Tell me always of them in yr letters. Bless you. Adieu. Increase & multiply & believe me to be

yr affectionate brother,
M. Fitzh Monk.

LETTER VI

From MAUGER F. MONK, Mussoorie Seminary,

To HUGH MONK, Guernsey.

[Endorsed:] "Per Overland Mail via Marseilles. Hugh Monk Esq, R.N. Ann's Place, St. Peter's Port, Guernsey, Channel Isles." "Landour September 15 12As." "12 Nov. 1840" "Answered Feby 21 1841"

13 SEPTEMBER 1840

My Dear Father,

Your kind letter of the 24th June last reached me on the 4th instant, the mail from the Red Sea having been delayed for want of steamers, and I need scarcely say how gladly was the sight of your handwriting welcomed after so long a period of estrangement; nor can I agree with you in thinking it at all less plain than it used to be, for I managed to read every word of it from beginning to end, tho' the rain or mayhap the salt-water had done all that was practicable toward effacing it, so much so that the postscript written in some female hand, & which I judged to be that of one of my dear sisters, was totally illegible. I cannot thank you sufficiently for the affectionate delicacy which has forborne from all allusion to the gross misconduct of my youthful days, but I felt it keenly, my mind from reflection, remorse and the effects of climate has become diseased, and subjects me on occasions of excitement to a nervousness I have great difficulty in controlling. A much longer residence in the plains with the simple routine of military duty to perform would probably have made me a physical coward, perhaps worse. A moral coward you know I have always been. Blame me not then, my dearest father, if from want of energy I push not on so rapidly as you might expect me to do. To regain your esteem and the place I have lost in your affections would & will do much; my advancement must be very gradual, those about me must never know that I have been a soldier. I cannot endure scorn, & the public of India are a sneering race—far more so than any community I have witnessed—a beggarly race of exclusives who have their own hotels, to which none but civil or military servants can be admitted, & in Calcutta they have schools, in which no children but their own reside & are educated. They associate not even with the uncovenanted servants of the Honble Compny, for the most part men of superior talents, good circumstances, & undoubtedly the most efficient body in the pay of John Company.

My oriental studies are I regret to say much neglected, not thro' idleness, but from want of time. Six hours daily attendance in school, with three large classes to instruct in Latin, writing and arithmetic and twice a week an additional hour and a half teaching drawing; besides exercises to correct and subjects to set out of schoolhours give me but little leisure of my own and that while daylight lasts I avail myself of to take a little exercise. Mackinnon however gives me every credit for my exertions and I have now entered into a fresh agreement with him, which from & after the month of February next will considerably increase my income, probably in addition to my fixed salary of £20 per month (which begins to take effect from that month) about £15 or £20 more. All drawing pupils above twelve & the fee for the whole of the French scholars are to be mine. As he furnishes frames for the copies & pencils he reserves the twelve to cover his expenses. The instruction in both branches is to be given twice a week & he has willingly consented to let me limit the instruction in the Classics,

History etc to four times in the week. For the female members of his family he pays most liberally, giving me 12 Rs per month each for their instruction in drawing. Our good but worldly-minded Old Bishop, who visited the establishment some two or three months ago, gave me great praise for my scholars' progress & attainments; he examined the classes very strictly and there was no time for drilling them, his coming being wholly unexpected.

I have written to my dear Aunt Mauger & enclosed her my measures, requesting her subject to your consent to send me two suits of "Cloth Clothes", London made, & three or four pair of trowsers, double-milled. We can get no good cloth here & even if we could, the native Schneiders cannot make it up. The sleeve of a coat which cost 64 Rs parted from it a fortnight ago as I was mounting my poney to return from church; it is perfect misery to sit two hours in one of them; & we are obliged to be well-dressed, the school & play-ground (by far the largest piece of level ground in the settlement) being the fashionable lounge from one year's end to the other of the Bengal Sanatorium. I insist, however, on being allowed to pay for them myself, & tho' I ask you, my dear father, to advance me the first amount, let the bill be sent to me that I may know what sum I have to pay & what it will be necessary to remit for a similar supply yearly.

The Wellesley was in the Hoogly in March & I have heard indirectly that Henry waited on Coll Whish, but his letter, for I cannot but suppose that he wrote to me has never come to hand. Sara's letter, telling me of his coming out to join the Wellesley in the Childers had not then reached me. I have written to him however & anticipated your wishes on the subject of advice. To this letter dated 4th July, I have as yet received no answer. Accept my best, my most grateful thanks, my dearest father, for your great kindness, for the readiness with which you have granted far more than I should ever have asked. To my dearest sisters I will send my thanks by the next mail. In the meantime give each from me a kiss of true brotherly affection. May they long be a blessing to you. May you yet live to see those, who should have been so but alas are not, turn from the errors of their ways and become a comfort to your declining years. And I pray God that when I swerve from the right path or relax in my efforts to become a worthy member of society, the misery I have caused a too kind, too indulgent parent may be present to spur me, as it has hitherto done, to honorable exertion. To Magrath, to dear Sarah & her hopeful progeny let not my kindest regards & remembrances be wanting, and lovingly greet my Uncles & Aunts for me. For the sake of his family I trust Davy will have strength of mind to give up habits which alas I know how much it requires to conquer. Lambe's malady is of too old a standing to be now curable. Believe me to be, my Dear Father,

Your affectionate & would be again beloved son,
M. F. M.

LETTER VIV

From MAUGER MONK, Mussoorie
To ISABELLA MONK, Guernsey.
Per Overland Mail via Marseilles.
Stamped: 8 Jan 1841.

15 NOVEMBER 1840

My own Belle,

My most charitable & kindest of sisters, you have found an excuse for my egotism then let the following plead for my not writing you last month. There were too many letters en route, to answer one or two, tho' by the bye No.2 did not reach me in time for October's mail, I have now three of yours before me & one of Margaret's. The history of your travels is still on its voyage possibly between Singapore & Calcutta. I hope one from Harry will accompany it: he has been long in the East & has never yet written me at least no letter from him has ever reached me. No news as yet of the Madagascar, tho' I doubt not she is by this time in the Hooghly. I leave all, however, to Mr. O'Brien & expect the case by the latter end of January. Your letters, in fact, all from home, are to me an inexpressible source of pleasure; from the 20th to the end of every month, I look with intense anxiety for the arrival of the Bombay Mail & am superlatively happy for at least a week.

The boys of my own classes (sharp little scamps) observe the excessive elevation of my spirits at that time, calculate upon escaping duffings for some days &, I will do them the justice to say, take no advantage, they are, if possible, more diligent & anxious to please me. Tho' my existence is one of unvarying monotony I derive the greatest satisfaction from the thankfulness with wh many of them receive instruction at my hands, all are orderly & respectful, very many grateful for the little attention I can shew them; the more so perhaps from contrast; for the head master (the Burra Sahib) is of a most irascible temper & sometimes very harsh. It would do your little heart good to see them on their return from a visit, always with a bouquet of flowers for Mr. Monk & while they are in season I get one daily from their own little gardens. Pardon this digression. Let me hear, as you have promised, monthly by the overland mail, either from yourself or so[me] one at home. The danger incurred in sending letters by private hand is very great in India; the post office prosecute most unrelentingly, always suing for full penalties. Another inconvenience may arise from several letters directed to persons of the same name being put into the post at the same time. Only think of the clerk of the Calcutta office, receiving from Mr.Lacy two letters for me & two for Henry at the same time, casting his eye over the first & finding the name "Monk" on all scratches "Mussoorie" in large letters on the back of the four & bundles them all up to me thus preventing poor Hal receiving his despatches for at least one month. In future direct to me "Mr. Monk, Mussoorie (in large letters) Bengal" & no more & as the Indian dâk officers complain sadly of the letters sticking together from the use of wax, seal only with a wafer or one of those pretty little medallions Papa used on his last letter. Shd I make no comment on the melancholy occurrences, wh it is sometimes your painful task to mention as subjects of mournful interest or wh it is fitting that I shd be made acquainted with (such for instance as the melancholy death of poor Tom Guerin or the unfortunate break down in Mr. Davey's business, wh I am however happy to hear he is in a fair way of retrieving) deem me not unfeeling. The period, wh has elapsed between your writing & the receipt of my answer, has served to calm those painful feelings, wh it is the peculiar privilege & blessing of time to allay, & any recurrence on my part to the subject wd but recall.

On the step taken by William I can make no observation. As we approached manhood we saw & heard too little of each other to have made our views a subject of common interest, & as we have never corresponded (the fault if such it be was not mine my many letters remain unanswered to this day) as men we know nothing of each other. The step, wh I took to separate myself from all the ties humanity holds dear, but at the same time to wean myself from habits, wh could only end in irretrievable destruction & infamy, cost me a severe struggle. My probation has mentally been of the most severe description; even now my hours of reflection in the midst of abundant employment both of mind & body, are of a most painful character, not however without benefit. Not possessed of natural energy, I have by habit induced a power of resistance, a sort of moral negative, wh if it impels not forward, can at least enable me to resist temptation; a better instance of wh I cannot give than my newly formed determination not to marry, at least, for some years, as my dear father & she, whose good opinion I most regard next to his, my dearest Aunt William, seem wholly to disapprove of such a step. I sincerely trust, then that William may derive much benefit from the step he has taken as I cannot give him credit for acting without a motive.

You ask if I have fallen in with any old acquaintances. Were I to say no, I shd tell you a falsehood, but I have sought none & never been recognised. I once made a military salute (squared my elbow) to Bernard Kendall, but never made myself known to him. The condition of Indian society is such that they could not notice you, & I wish not to put those disposed to serve an old friend to the inconvenience of patronising, particularly where their own share of patronage may be scanty enough to aid their own views of advancement. Some of my old schoolfellows have been in my neighbourhood at different times, but I have pursued the same line of conduct. A similar reason has prevented me waiting on Mrs. Bellew (Anne Jeremie that was) tho' she resided some time at Mussoorie.

Magrath's arm & his bodily ailment arising from the puncture are, I suppose, well now, & will, by the time this reaches you have been totally forgotten. Tho' I regret the cause, I really don't think a little extra bustle can be productive of aught but benefit to my poor dear old father, whose habits have ever been of a most active description. It won't do for him to have no occupation, he'd very soon die of pure ennui. Give my kindest regards to him, Magrath, I mean. Sarah, whom I am most happy to hear, bears up well with her increasing family. Tho' many are absent, your Christmas party with the bairns (Heaven's fairest blessings on them) will not be so very small. How I shd like to see the young ones enjoy their plum-pudding, Henry of course on Grand-papa's right prattling away to the amusement of all, Hugh's [Miles?] large eyes glistening with delight, Johnny with his spoon almost as big as his own head & napkin under his chin besmearing his pretty cheeks each time he wd fill his mouth, the lovely little Ellen (a good many lovely Ellens in Mussoorie and some Helens too) as amiable as pretty & Master Chas Frederic struggling in his mother's lap to catch a stray plate or wine glass & fling it on the floor.

A merry Christmas may you all enjoy & see many succeeding ones. Shd my plans, at present in embryo, not be necessarily altered, don't be surprised at my taking a Xmas dinner five years hence with you all, even suppose you get a good husband before then I wish with all my heart you may! As you are not sporting people at home I shall not entertain you with a shooting excursion I took during the few days holidays, wh succeeded our examination last month; but I hope in the course of a month or two to send home some sketches of the neighbourhood, perhaps a dozen wh I shd be glad to have published, if my dear old father will join me in a piece of speculation, on wh subject I wish you to sound him as well as to ascertain for me, what number of copies can be struck off each stone.

The expence of lithography cannot be very great and somewhere between 200 & 300 copies wd remunerate me handsomely, enable me to purchase a piece of ground & with what I can save, build a nice little house. This house wd give me at least 20 per cent most probably 25 & when built I cd raise sufft on it to build another at 8 per cent making any way a clear profit of 12 or 14 per cent & these same two little houses wd at any time render me independent of the caprices of my present employer, who, tho' a good man in the main, is of a most disagreeable temper one, in fact, wh few persons can put up with. Fancy, a house here with only three rooms, that wd cost about £250 or £300 building will let for £60 the season: no mistake, rent paid in advance & the tenant liable for all damage by fire. The sale of whatever other number of copies were struck off ought to defray all expenses with interest on the money laid out. You must not, my dearest Bell, expend your pocket allowance upon me, for much as I should have enjoyed Nichs Nickleby, from wh I have read many extracts, it wd have grieved me to receive ought I knew you cd not well afford—the more especially as I cod send nothing from here worth your acceptance. I have had two neat little cases made, one for you, the other for Aunt Wm and when the butterfly season comes round again shall employ natives to bring me the most beautiful specimens the Himalaya will produce & send them to England by some of my scholars. Quant aux livres when I can send, a remittance I shall also send a list of books I wd wish sent to me. My light reading is at present confined to the works of Voltaire, Racine etc, to fit myself for my additional duty as teacher of the French language. Only listen to the enumeration of my titles to come in force from after the lst of Feby next: Hd Classical Master, Professor of French, Drawing & Fencing at Mussoorie Seminary. My salary as the first will keep me comfortably. The profits derived from the latter are all to be put by in the Agra Bank, till wanted. And now, my own dearest sister, I must close this letter wh is not so interesting as it shd be, the fact is, my love, yesterday afternoon I spent in shooting, an amusement I can only enjoy on occasional half-holidays, such as Saturday afternoon is with us, & having over exerted myself, I have been bothered all day with a splitting headache. Three of Dr. Grierson's pills are lying on the table intended to be taken at bedtime, their smell reminds me of home:- they have much the same delicious odour as Papa used to dose us with, as in many other things the remedy is nauseous enough, but we mind not that, if the effect be what is desired. My best love to Margaret, tell her my [sic] fat Madge that our holidays wh last for six weeks commence this day month when I promise to sit down & write all the funny anecdotes of Indian life I am able to recall. It won't do to tell any more to Aunt Wm, she tells me, plump & plain, that she makes every allowance for a traveller & will not give full credence to my stories. God bless you my dearest sister, my dear father, brothers & sisters, to whom all filial & fraternal love & regard from

Your sincerely attached brother,
M Fitzh Monk.

P.S. Don't forget the usual allowance of compliments & kind regards to all inquiring friends. I sent Uncle & Aunt Wm theirs two months ago & remind Papa of the foils I mentioned in my letter to him, Solengen blades—the lightest procurable, hilts guards, masks & gloves. Case not to exceed 30 lbs. I have ordered a few from Calcutta in the mean time. Excuse mistakes, bad writing, want of interesting matter, egotism etc. etc. my head aches & I cannot defer writing. To-morrow's post will be last safe one, for the mail leaves Bombay Dec lst. Adieu, a merry Xmas.

HIMALAYAN CLASSICS MASTER 1841-1842

LETTER VIII

From MAUGER MONK, Mussoorie

To HUGH MONK, Guernsey.

[Endorsed:] "Per Overland Mail via Falmouth. Hugh Monk Esq., Surgeon R.N., Ann's Place, Guernsey, Channel Isles.".

"Landour 15 January 1841. Paid 12 Ans"

14 JANUARY 1841

My Dearest Father,

The government official notification of an intention to dispatch a mail overland towards the end of Dec reached this remote station too late to permit my availing myself of it:- indeed we hardly expected that Mehemet Ali would have used that forbearance towards the English Government, which it appears he has so generously shown & allowed the Indian letter bags to cross his beleaguered country. As it is, so doubtful were the authorities in the Mediterranean of the practicability of sending the mail across the desert that the one containing my dear sister Margery's letter was forwarded via Trebizond.

We are now in the midst of our Christmas vacation (the only one in the year) & tho' I am but just returned from a ten days trip to the valley of the Dhoon at the foot of the hills, have been very busy preparing for the opening of the campaign on the lst Febry, as I then expect a considerable number of drawing pupils & a fair sprinkling of French ones. The latter are to be my sole perquisite, for drawing, I am to receive the fees for all above twelve,

Mr. Mackinnon taking the amount paid for that number & supplying materials. The charge is but 5 Rs per month, but the number of pupils will be increased owing to its being so moderate. When my foils &c arrive from Calcutta I shall commence teaching fencing but only to a limited number, & at a much higher rate. I have requested my dear Bell to trouble you with a commission which I hope you will be kind enough to execute for me, & get such foils as may be suitable for mere boys, the more so, as the lads born in this country are physically weaker in nine cases out of ten than those of a corresponding age at home but whatever you are kind enough to procure for me I must be allowed to pay for, that is a sine quâ non. I have already drawn too much upon you, my dear Father, to the prejudice I much fear of my poor sisters' education to accept any thing more at your hands tho' to be still unreasonable & qualify my assertion, there is one gift I should most highly prize. A trip to Paris next summer is, it has been whispered to me, in contemplation. Should my dear father go, would it not be practicable to get one of the many talented but needy artists of the French capital to paint a moderate sized portrait in oil of him, & should the additional expense not be great, to include in the same picture my two sisters to complete a group. Such a present would be indeed a treasure to me—an ever present memento of my past misconduct & an encouragement to strive daily more & more to make myself worthy of the parent I have done so much to harass & grieve. Tho' I have hinted to my dear Isabella the possibility of my one day revisiting Guernsey & that ere many years have elapsed, I much fear that my tent must be pitched in the "clime of the sun" & very many circles revolved round that luminary before I shall be in a situation to set eyes on the isle of my birth. When framed the picture could be easily packed so as to reach me without being injured. In return, as soon as my box arrives, I hope, as my leisure time permits, to be able to forward a few views of the Himalayas, particularly of the school & that part of the range of which I am now a denizen.

My boxes arrived safe at Calcutta & as Mr. O'Brien assures me uninjured. He sent them by steam to Allahabad, which place they reached on the 16th Dec & will probably be here on the 8th Feby. A hundred rupees will, I believe, cover the expenses of carriage. Mussoorie is most probably not laid down in any map of India you possess, but as it was for a time within two miles of the Hd Qrs of the Revenue Survey I can give you its exact bearings. Long: 78° 3′ East, Lat: 30° 28′ 29″ North, distance from Calcutta about 1040 miles, from which place the mail is twelve days on its road but only nine from Bombay. Thus news from England reaches us three days earlier than it gets to the capital, which is twelve days dâk from Bombay.

No news has reached us yet of any importance from China beyond the occupation of Chusan & the audience appointed by the Emperor to hear the complaints of the barbarians, nor has any letter from Henry ever come to hand. We have heard of the bombardment of Beyrout & the ferment among the French; wars & rumours of wars seem to be the order & topic of the day. The Afghanistan campaign is nearly at an end. Dost Mahomed is on his road to India as a prisoner, but with all the pomp & parade of a noble & fallen prince. He is to be pensioned by the company & sent to reside at the new hill station of Darjeeling at the foot of the Naipaul range. An attack is meditated on Lahore, the kingdom of the Indian one-eyed Hannibal, the late Runjeeh Sing. From its locality this country is generally known by the name of the Punjaub, or five rivers. The Naipaulese are alarmed at the preparations made against them: & for the present they have cried, 'Peccavimus'; their character is however so restless & warlike that a lasting peace is not expected till Company Bahadoor's Sepoys are occupying their capital Catmandoo. My old troop is gone a second time against a refractory Rajah, whom the very rattle of our gunwheels brought to his senses last year without our having occasion even to unlimber for action. I know we felt much disappointed at marching back without firing a shot, for the Nawab is reported wealthy & we then expected a good share of what Blucher used to call "blunder" tho' but little of it falls to the lot of the artilleryman except those of the spiking party.

I ought to have written to Magrath & Margaret, but have only this one sheet of thin paper. An eight-mile ride would enable me to get some, had I time without fear of losing the dâk. My best love to them & they shall hear from me by the next mail. All fraternal love & kisses to Sarah & Bell, nor forget to bestow a kiss of affection from Uncle Mauger on each of her smiling bairns. Without knowing much of the matter I think it almost time that she should stop breeding for a season. To my uncles, aunts & real friends commend me most affectionately. That you may enjoy good health & be spared to us for many years to come is the sincere prayer of

Your affectionate son
M. Fitzh. Monk.

LETTER IX

From MAUGER MONK, Mussoorie
To MARGARET MONK, Ann's Place, Guernsey.
Per Overland Mail, via Falmouth.

12 FEBRUARY 1841

My Dearest Sister Margaret,

[Thanks for presents sent & received, in overblown, flowery & partly maudlin style.] In particular, tell Papa that I trust I shall ever treasure as I ought the kind memento he has sent me of my poor dear mother. Everything arrived safe & uninjured having never been opened after they left England. On comparing the list with the articles, *Tacitus* (in Latin) was the only book I did not find but that is no matter, as I do not want it. The pretty portrait of our queen adorns my mantlepiece in a heavy walnut frame, in fact my snug little sitting-room is become quite a handsome library, & thanks to you all, I have more personal ornaments than wd satisfy the greatest dandy in the Himalaya, of our portion of wh I hope in the course of a few months to send home some sketches. Little spare time, however, falls to my lot: I have plenty of work &, as my health is excellent, find infinitely more comfort & happiness in employment than in idleness. With every thing around me so fresh from Europe, you must not be surprised if my thoughts are continually reverting homewards, & that indulging in a reverie as I mix my nightcap at 11 o'clock (the regular hour) I afterwards retire to bed to dream of schemes for enabling me to revisit at an early day the sweet little "isle, where Flora's smile" &c, of the impracticability of wh plain-matter-of-fact day-light too sensibly convinces me ... [Re gifts] I look not upon them as a reward for my first step but as a stimulus to greater exertion. Mr. Mathew Goodwin's instrument will be only useful to me as a protractor:- it is at least sixty years old. The instruments in use in the school are the latest improvements of Troughton & Simms, the first mathematical instrument makers in the world, & with one of those, I cd do a good day's work at surveying, before the old-fashioned Theodolite of Adams could be even levelled & with twenty-five times the accuracy. In these days of Trigonometrical Surveying we make our calculations to the decimal of a second. I hope his charge was a conscientious one.

We opened the school campaign, a more successful one than that of Afghanistan to us masters, as we are always the thrashing party, yet shed no blood, on the lst Feb with a strong prospect of increasing numbers so I have popped my gun into its case, my dogs into their kennel, & shall only have occasion for my mountain steed (hairy as a wild Ukraine courser & sure-footed as a chamois) to ride to church on Sundays. We had only one night's fall of snow, wh melted too rapidly to compel the bear's [sic] to quit their fastnesses, & I was too busy preparing drawings & polishing my French to quit my post for any length of time:- so got but one Bruin, who showed no fight, having been brained by the first bullet. He furnished five quart bottles of excellent grease & two splendid hams but his coat was too much torn by his fall among the rocks to be worth preserving. I dined with Mr. & Mrs. Mackinnon both Xmas & New Year's day nor did we forget our friends, relations & kinsfolk across the Herring Pond, as the sailors call it, & ended our evenings with a review of the Progress of the Arts & Sciences in Europe, with wh our credulity can hardly keep pace, & tho' we touched on the times & the signs thereof, found ourselves too matter-of-fact to hazard any possible calculations as to what even the next quarter century might bring forth.

[Little news from China & nothing from Harry.]

I had treasured up some of my choice military anecdotes for my dear Madge, but don't like now to commit them to paper, they'll keep well & serve to amuse the nephews and nieces as I sit in the ingle-nook with my pipe (I can't get over the tobacco you see) & pot of home brew'd on my return to Europe to claim yr hospitality. [Remembrances to aunts & uncles etc.] When you write again, may I venture' to suggest a leetle news respecting some of my old schoolfellows. What is Corbin doing? Whither has Johnny Cartwright gone? Shd Aunt Eliza be communicative a word or two about Mr. Pym & young Lockyer of Plymouth wd be acceptable. The latter must by this time have run thro' his money, & be ripe for the Bengal Arty. I see by the stars that Fredk Lukis is a great man in the Mechanics Institute. What arc John & Wm engaged upon? Dick Goodwin appears to be assisting his father but what have become of poor Mr. Jos Collings's sons? Isn't Augy somewhere in India? Young Symons is I know, but it's all my eye about his being wounded at Khelat. The 2nd or Queen's (his regimt) were to have led the storming party at Ghuzmi. Pretty set of bunglers! They let the 13th Light Infy, the Bengal European Regt & the 48th N.I.—blackies—take the town before they cd form up, Lord Keane, who got his title for the gallantry & skill of a Bengal Engineer officer, Major Thomson (not for any act of his own) gave them great soap but the Afghanistan campaign added very little to the honours of the 2nd, as all here know.

I wish I cd send you & Bell something more tangible than my sincerest love & affection. My Tindale shall go to Hurdwar fair in April, & tho' we can't yet afford a cashmere shawl a piece, we'll try and get something of that country wool, soft as down & smooth as mouse's skin, to make you each a warm cloak ...

LETTER X

From MAUGER MONK, Mussoorie
To SARAH MAGRATH, Pollet Street, Guernsey.
Per Overland Mail via Falmouth.

12 FEBRUARY 1841

My Dearest Sarah,

A choir of young Christians, a sick husband to nurse & a daily allowance of nauseous mixtures to compound speak too plainly of yr manifold occupations to require an apology for not writing sooner. Besides, come the letter when it may, it is ever highly welcome.

Egad! My application to the Commander-in-Chief for permission to take a wife, shd fortune throw one in my way upon whom I cod condescend to bestow myself, seems to have placed me in a complete cross-fire; Ann's Place first, Clapton next & lastly the Pollet have opened battery upon me, so that I was almost annihilated. Staggered I certainly was, & am lucky in not having you all at hand to profit by my confusion! N'aie donc pas de peur, ma chère soeur, when I take a wife I don't mean to take an encumbrance. I don't intend to enlist under the banner of Hymen till I am well able to maintain Mrs. M or I find a Mrs. M. F. M able to maintain me. You know economy is not one of my failings. I am too well quit of the first enlistment to engage a second time in a service, whence four hundred rupees & a memorial to the commander of the forces, wd not purchase my discharge. When I made my application I had not been long from the plains of India, where the seventh commandmt is not considered as part of the decaloque, & the breach of the tenth, the simple coveting is in most cases rapidly followed by the "walking off bodily with". You may tell Nicholas that saleable ladies with ropes round their necks fetch a better price here than in Smithfield market. Fancy a comrade of mine, offering me his wife, a fresh & very pretty importation from Limerick for 35 rupees & a case-bottle of Grog! As you may suppose, I declined the purchase—possession was all very well, but I don't admire property in live stock.

I am exceedingly glad to hear that Magrath got so well over his puncture & its effects tho' he appears to have been laid up for some time & in some danger from all accounts. It won't do for him or you to part company yet a while. A buxom widow with five incumbrances, angels tho' they be, wd stand but a small chance in the Indian Market of picking up a second husband so at home I look upon her case as hopeless. No. 2 wd doubtless be regarded as a merciful dispensation of providence. May you be long spared to each other, & have baskets full of children, as the old Irish soldiers always wind up their tales. Au moins, you don't seem to care how many there are, if you settle so easily in yr own mind the serving out two boys to each of yr brothers, for I presume from yr having honoured me with two it is yr intention to be equally generous to Will, & the Chinaman.

For my own part, believing as I do that I am not fated to transmit to posterity the hereditary honours of the Monks [in fact, he was the only one of three brothers who did], I shall at some future day, if I gain caste in India, be most happy to do my best for the lads but if you find either of them inclined to take spade, hammer or chisel in his fist & become a practical and theoretical mechanic, don't let any false notions of pride on yr part thwart him. It strikes me very forcibly that civil engineers, canal & road manufacturers & architects are the men; whom India wants. These departments have been too long in the hands of the army, to the great deterioration of military duties, habits & discipline, to let them remain so much longer. The sipahis will soon have to resume their swords, for seat me pretty considerably particularly tarnation high on Dhawal-Ghiri during a frosty night if they won't soon want 'em, & then hurrah for those qualified to step into the, if necessity, vacated civil employment. In their education make the classics an entirely secondary consideration. Ground them well in arithmetic, geometry & the sciences, & let the bent of their own inclinations follow out their own course. They'll soon choose for themselves. A doctor, lawyer & parson you of course intend to have in the family. Make interest for an East Indian Chaplaincy for the last, he'll get good pay & only very moderate work while in the country & a major's pension, when that work is done. Train these three up according to the most approved fashion, but mind & keep pace with the march of intellect. There now is a lot of unpaid for advice, wh you may follow or not as you please. I'm not answerable for it with a fee.

As you all seem to calculate upon my paying you a visit some day without my ever leading you to think it possible, I shd very much like to know what has put that notion into yr heads? If I do get a chance it won't be for the next four years; for at present I don't see wh way to steer my course, so as to get well beyond my present station in society. I think the Moonshee & I must rub up the neglected Persian & Hindustanee, so that shd I return I may eke out a livelihood by the somewhat precarious profession of professor of Oriental languages.

At present I have nothing more to say & think I have scribbled enough nonsense. The receipt of the presents, (books, bijouterie, instruments etc) so kindly sent me from home have been acknowledged, I trust, gratefully. Accept my best thanks for the "Suns" you have sent me but pray don't send any more. We have too much sun in India. In truth I have no time to look into them &

can't afford a pound a month postage for them. Fact 'pon honour, not yet quite clear of expenses of discharge & outfits. Living up here twice as expensive as in the plains. Hills-oxless: mutton, scraggy & dear: corn & grain all carried up on men's back—25 per cent upon every thing in consequence—no competition in the bazaars, all pull together, so the sahibs suffer. Shall be very glad of a good weekly paper containing reviews, literary & scientific notices, arts & artists & all them ere sort of things. Will contrive to read it: don't care about police reports, feel ashamed of having figured in them myself & abominate murders, sudden deaths, accidents & advertisements.

[Usual messages to relations, including nephews.] Glad you told me their names, tho' I remembered all but Miles's thought he was called Hugh. Clap me down for godfather of the next. Give my most sincere regards to Nicholas: tell him I shan't deceive him in his expectations of me. I believe he always thought well of me, even when my credit was below low-water mark. As for you, why my old Staff-Sergt's blessing on the Colonel, when he got him promoted to a Sub-Conductorship to you, "May yer honour never die in childbed or any other bed, so long life to yer honour & yr honour's lady." God bless you. Adieu ...

LETTER XI

From MAUGER MONK, Mussoorie
To ISABELLA MONK, Ann's Place, Guernsey.
Per Overland Mail via Falmouth.

9 APRIL 1841

My Dearest Bell,

[Because he has not heard from Guernsey in the last two mails, he speculates, guiltily, on what he has done to cause their silence. He defends his own failure to write every mail on the grounds of not knowing till the last minute when the mail is going, and of interruption of posts by tigers.] No less than three [runners] have perished in this way since Xmas at a dismal defile called Keeree about 25 or 20 miles from the foot of our range. The Dhoon of Deyrah, a rich plain extending from this to the Eastern range abounds in Royal Bengals, wh yearly afford great sport to the tiger killers of the North. One of the best known of these, Judge Okeden [?], has purchased an estate up here on wh I believe, he intends residing preparatory to his return to Europe. Many of these ferocious brutes (the tigers I mean) have great opportunities of indulging their preference (after they have once tasted it) for human blood at this season of the year. Many of the visitors to Hurdwar fair, both going & returning annually become their prey, & this year they may expect a great blow out; for the male fair, wh occurs only once in twelve years, takes place this: the intermediate annual ones are termed female, so you may judge of the gallantry of those who dwell in the land "where the virgins are soft as the roses they twine." Faugh! I wish they didn't stink so of cocoa-nut oil, or were troubled with a second idea. As for the roses, take a walk in Guernsey market on a Saturday morning & you will see & smell far more beautiful & fragrant ones than you will in Bengal. I wod strongly recommend any one coming to India to leave all romance at home & endeavour to forget as soon as possible all that they have read in the poets, about the "land of the Sun". ... But I don't mean to run India down. Why shod I? We've not quarelled. It's a deuced fine place for a real matter-of-fact man— a character the most sure to astonish the natives. No matter; revenons à nos moutons—the fair at Hurdwar, to wh I shod have liked to have gone, but knew it was no use asking leave, as we get no holidays at Easter. This fair, the largest in the East, is visited by merchants from all parts of the continent of Asia, & the traffic carried on, both in buying, selling & barter is immense. The horses brought by the Turcomans & other tribes are said to be of the most beautiful kind & another saleable article, the slave-ladies, are all selected from the most beautiful of the Eastern races. Ten thousand rupees for a Circassian wife is paying a tolerable sum for the ornamental. Here the useful is never combined with the agreable. The sight, however, of Hurdwar at this time has been described to be & must be as beautiful as novel. Consider the various garb, ranks, characters & nations that one meets with there, the immense & rich variety of goods & the swarms of pilgrims who come to bathe in the spot where the sacred Ganges first issues into the plains after a headlong descent from its source of near 20,000 ft & the imagination will at least portray a scene of great interest.

Enough of India for the present! My mind must now revert to Europe as I have a job or two that I wish you to do for me. In primis, let me have, if possible, a copy of Mr. Arago's lecture on the inventions of Daguerre & Niepce, give me your own opinion of them (for the Daguerre type has, I see, been exhibited in Guernsey), ascertain what improvements have been made on the invention in England, whether any chemically-prepared paper has been substituted for the copper plates, & having obtained all the information on the principle & practice of the Daguerre system that you can, let me know the cost of a complete set of apparatus of a modest size, in short, if not too expensive, send me one, I know I cod turn many a gold mohur by it.

And lastly, it strikes me very forcibly that this new republic of New Zealand will be a fine field for an adventurer like me. I much fear that the prejudices of caste, the cursed distinctions between covenanted & uncovenanted servants will ever prove an insurmountable bar to regaining a lost position in society in India & if you will kindly furnish me with data, (mind a plain & unvarnished tale) on wh to fix some principle of action I'll be off there either next cold season or that of 1842. I have some knowledge of Hobson, the governor but don't feel disposed to try His Excellency, till I have positive information on wh I can act, & the approval of my friends at home. So, my dearest Bell, as the restless devil of the family is on a visit, let me have all the information you, my dear Papa, or Magrath can get, but let me know your authorities & if in print, send me the original. I like much the notion of a popular government, tho' at present decidedly oligarchal in my political creed. Physically I am very strong; & from habit, active & tho' wanting in strength of mind & perseverance, think that I still possess sufficient qualifications to use in a settlement such as New Zealand has been described to me. Adieu, ma très chère, if I get no letters this overland I shall be au désespoir ...

P.S. I began this on the 9th & closed it on the 15th inst but have not as yet heard from China. I hope you have been more favoured.

The government are proposing to send home two mails monthly, overland. Don't I wish they may do it!

Ghoont, *the obstinate but agile mule was the preferred form of transport in these hills*

LETTER XII

From MAUGER MONK, Mussoorie
To HUGH MONK, Guernsey.
[Endorsements: same as 37, plus]: "Landour '41 May 9 Paid 12 An."

9 MAY 1841

My Dearest Father,

Your letter of the 21st Feb was a most welcome one. I had received none by either of the two preceding mails, & was completely on the fidget fearing that none might arrive by April's dâk. The kindness and readiness, with which you have complied with every wish of mine, almost convince me of my selfishness in preferring requests & I sincerely regretted that my letter to Isabella, which had left the hills seven days previous to the arrival of yours, contained a commission, without forwarding the wherewithal to execute it. Tho' not many years in India, I must be blind indeed not to perceive that "money is power" that by its aid almost any thing is to be acquired & I have become so far bitten with the Anglo-Indian mania, as to be positively striving to conquer my nature, lavish, as you have too good cause to know it to be & become a selfish, pice-scraping Indian. I asked for a Daguerrotyperama, to coin a word, knowing the rage for novelty among the ladies of the East, who delight in beer-shraub & scandal & the readiness with which works of art, owing to their scarceness, are bought up. The same desire of power, or rather of rendering myself independent in the selection of future employment, (which of some kind or other a man who can read and write need never be without) induced the suggestion of publishing a few views of the hills, & the teaching fencing. Future employment! This requires to you some explanation, as it implies a probability of my leaving Mr. Mackinnon & leave him I certainly shall, the very moment I can find a better situation after the fulfilment of my agreement. To tell you the way in which the actions & movements of his European assistants are controlled, the privacy of domestic life completely broken in upon, by your own or your neighbours servants being pumped & truckled with; your every look, your every action canvassed, as tho' it were likely to prejudice the interests of the establishment, would satisfy you that no purely independent spirited fellow would stand such treatment for an hour, & no adventurous citizen of the world, like myself, longer than it suited his own views. The man who "sits in the high places" (Mackinnon I mean) & I have quarrelled much of late, & are just now what is usually, but not classically termed, "damned civil to each other". Excuse the expression I can find no other to describe so well our respective positions. At present it suits me not to leave him, or him to part with me. My place is not easily filled, & my progress must be in the ascendancy scale. I must not withdraw my foot after having once placed it on the ladder step. What interest my pupils' parents possess they are sure in this every-one-for-himself community to need & use only for themselves. Official Residencies are the especial perquisites of field officers & civil covenanted servants:- secretaryships in all, save the military departments, of the latter. Deputy Collectorships are open to all candidates, overseerships of public works, & military & civil offices as clerks. In all these, however, there is one great drawback. Respected you may be, but will never be looked on as a gentleman, & have the mortification of finding yourself on an equality with the half-caste, half-educated country-borns, &

often less regarded than the native shroffs or soucars, the money-managers, in whose power it not infrequently happens that the head man is. Coll Everest, the head of the Trigonometrical Survey is the only chef de department I know, who treats his clerks with any degree of gentlemanly civility, & to him I should certainly offer myself, but that he leaves for Europe in October, & the salary for the first seven years will do no more than support one. My only European co-adjutor (Mr. Outhwaite) is of a good Yorkshire family, but enjoys very indifferent health, or he would be on his way to Engd. He is in fact too weak to cross India tho' he intends next cold season taking Egypt in his way home, &, if it appears a good one, entering the service of the Pacha, as a Cavalry officer. He purchased his own discharge out of the 16th Lancers, or rather, his friends at home did so & sent it out to him. He is continually plaguing me to go to Egypt with him, praising the country, the martial & energetic character of Mehemet & the Arabs, & instituting comparisons much to the disadvantage of India & the Hindoos. Were he a person I liked as a companion, I might be tempted but under existing circumstances shall be content to try India a little longer. He has charge of the 4th class (mine are the two first) & the boys below that are committed to the tender mercies of two snuff-coloured gents, whose language is none of the purest; & who, I very much suspect, are at the bottom of the espionage system, so avowedly carried on in the establishment & I imagine originally set on foot by the she-Mackinnon (a widow with two children when the Scotchman married her). They have added four to the two between them (one however deceased) & there is to all appearance another under weigh. Four days in the week, since the writing-master left, have I to be in the school-room nine hours a day, & the only emolument I derive from the extras is 15 Rupees monthly for my three French pupils. He keeps, I think purposely to annoy me, the number of drawing boys at 12, so from them I get nothing. All above, I was to have had. I know your aversion to a crossed letter, so shall bring this to a close, with a repetition of the thanks I expressed in my letter to you in Jany last for your kindness & liberality towards me. The boxes arrived perfectly safe & uninjured. Everything in fact in good order. May I show you by my exertions that I am sincerely grateful, & not slacken in my endeavours to rise. With kind love to Uncles Joseph & Wm. & Aunts Eliza, & Wm. & all fraternal affection to my dearest sisters & Magrath & sincere prayers that you may be long spared to us & see your sons turn out worthy of their father, I remain,

Your dutiful & most affectionate son,
Mauger.

P.S. I must not omit an avuncular kiss & blessing for Sarah's cherubs, which please to bestow for me; & tell the dear girls I shall cherish their coming presents for their sakes. No news yet from Harry;- Canton is taken, with a loss on our side of 2 killed & 17 slightly wounded. That of the Chinese is not known in killed & wounded. 1500 were made prisoners in pushing up the river; & 842 pieces of cannon destroyed, with the Chinese Lord High Admiral, who was cut in two by a shot, several mandarins killed; the Cambridge, an old Indiaman, on which they had mounted 34 guns and all their war-junks burnt. Adieu.

LETTER XIII

From MAUGER MONK, Mussoorie

To ISABELLA & MARGARET MONK, Guernsey.

Per Overland Mail via Falmouth.

13 AUGUST 1841

[He did not write last mail. Thanks for attending to his requests tho' the 'Roberts' has not arrived at Calcutta yet.]

The spring vessels are not uncommonly six months on the voyage. [The risk to the boxes en route from Calcutta to Mussoorie is] not near so great as you imagine. [Difficulties of corresponding with Hal in China.] The new Admiral & Plenipo are off for China, our relations with wh seem to be as much adrift as they were at the commencement of the war. The Afghan campaign appears to be, in the opinion of those at home, anything but a feather in Lord Auckland's cap & its occupation, or rather, that of Afghanistan a galling eyesore to the political economists being a drain on this country of upwards of 50 lacs, even if the whole annual revenue of that robber land were set in the balance against the expenditure, a thing impossible in its present unsettled state. One third can with difficulty be now collected. Each of your last letters were delicious treats, tho' they gave no flattering description of any of my old school fellows. Save that I pine for my station in society & long to see you all, once more, I envy them not in fact, I see nothing but the above causes, wh wd induce me to change places with them, tho' far, very far from being comfortable at present. Mackinnon &

I have not been on speaking terms for the last four months, owing, I fear, to some under hand reports wh I am but just now enabled to trace & hope by next dak to give you a fuller account of. The principal one I have just received a letter from the Commanding Officer at the convalescent depôt, fully rebutting. Woe to the mean-spirited scoundrel to whom I trace them. I'll make an example of him. However don't make yourselves uneasy about me; as I know of no act of mine of which, since I came to India, I have cause to be ashamed.

I am hard at work preparing for the examination & faith, the rising generation of India require great training. Be it owing to any Boeotian property in the air of this healthy region, or to any degeneracy in intellect in the Anglo-Indian breed, I know not, but they are incomparably duller than boys of equal ages at home.

The circumstances I have above mentioned, wh may possibly terminate in an action for libel, if I find any maligner worth powder & shot, prevent me remitting, as I intended, the money my dear father has been kind enough to advance, on my account, at least, for the present. With all my economy (no great portion, I see you say with a somewhat mournful smile) I have not yet many hundred rupees by me. I had wished to write to Uncle Will this month, but am not in the vein. Kindly communicate my good intent & nepotical love & ask him to ascertain for me the market price of musk either by the pod, pound or ounce, & let me know as early as possible together with the duty at home on its importation.

I think I can manage to send to Europe from 10 to 12 lbs of genuine musk yearly, if it will pay cent per cent. The bear's grease, pure as I know it to be, (being my own shooting, not the grease, but the bear) have [sic] failed in producing the whiskers, or stopping the greys from increasing. I send you a lock cut from behind & just above the ear as a specimen. I am almost as grey as my dear father was, when I last saw him. The unusually heavy & early monsoon has spoilt all my paper. I dare not attempt to cross this letter:- it wd be illegible.

The usual family greetings.

LETTER XIV

From MAUGER MONK, Mussoorie
To HUGH MONK, Guernsey.
[Endorsements: same as 37, plus]: "Answered Nov 22 per Falmouth."

14 SEPT 1841

My Dearest Father,

I have been vexed with myself for the last month at having written to Bell in the style I did by the last Overland. What business have I to trouble you with the petty annoyances I sometimes meet with, which are almost forgotten by the time an account of them reaches you, you to whom I am well assured, not only my best prospects, but present comfort are a source of happiness? My isolated situation is my best apology; the fumes of my ill-humour want a vent & having no friend, not even an acquaintance, to whom I would care to impart my petty griefs, I regret that I discharged my bile in the manner I did, bespattering all India, its society & its castes, because I had been unable to trace the author of certain calumnies, which I found were operating greatly to my prejudice as a schoolmaster—morally, I mean, not as to qualification. As I mentioned them in my last, I may now tell you the result of my inquiries, which have terminated in as unsatisfactory a manner as possible, save that it has afforded me an opportunity of clearing my character, the whole onus being thrown on a dead man, the Mr. Outhwaite I mentioned in my last letter to you as being the next assistant to myself, & in that to my sisters as being dead. That the lancer, which he had been, was trying to oust me, I have now no doubt, both from his own often expressed wish to have one of the higher classes and the proverbially treacherous character of all the Queen's Soldiers in India but I have reason to believe my worst calumniator is a half-negro assistant, the greatest sneak & like all sneaks, the most abject wretch I ever met with. He is really not worth kicking, unless it be down one of the precipices in the interior of the hills. The substance of the accusations against me are these, as far as I can find out for no one will now stand forward as my accuser: That, having during the period I was in the army lived in open adultery with a European woman, whom I had purchased from her husband, (the whole a most infamous fabrication) and having been a notoriously dissipated character, (in the face of the voluntary testimony of my own officers) & being then & still addicted to low company, (I have not made an acquaintance nor associated with a single individual since I came to Mussoorie) I was morally unfit for the situation of Head Assistant in an establishment for the education of youth. Had I been strictly economical I should have found myself in a situation to have left the seminary at the termination of my present agreement without troubling myself to refute any of the aspersions, which in any other capacity would not have been a feather's weight against me & it shall be my fault, if I do not leave at the termination of the period, to which I have extended my agreement, viz. Christmas 1842, unless things be very much altered. The renewal of my agreement will be a sufficient refutation to the public of the reports against my character, as it implies satisfaction in the head of the establishment, who is responsible to them & at the fall of the ensuing year I shall have saved enough to journey wherever I like. Calculating on a sojourn here of four or five years I laid out more than I ought in making myself snug & comfortable, but all I have purchased will, if necessary, be available to turn into cash. My present mode of life under the savage, in addition to the slavery & discomfort to which it subjects me, suits not my views, for as I mentioned before, I have not, since I came to Mussoorie made a single acquaintance, nor am I in any way thrown in contact with those, whom I should wish to know & whose patronage might be made available. Any eligible, but active, situation under government, with even an inferior salary, I shall gladly jump at, if it holds out a good prospect of future advancement & having on mature deliberation resolved on this, shall fit myself to be ready to enter as a candidate for anything, which may offer to my liking. I have now given you three pages of No.1, of whom I am, like all the world here, getting fonder than I ought, or at least, more careless of showing it, since the whole Indian community bear selfishness indelibly stamped both on their acts & brows. I hope the perusal of this wont cause any mischief to your eyes, which I sincerely regret to learn have been again attacked, & pray, let no anxiety on my account be the cause of any uneasiness to you. I shall not again offend you with a story of my petty cares. You, God knows, have had, & still have trouble enough with your scapegrace sons. May Heaven send them all speedy reformation & improvement. My kindest love & kisses to your sole comforts, the girls. Bless their dear hearts. Good husbands to them soon. I have had no correspondence with Coll Whish for some time. He is a psalm-singer & does not like to be bothered but I mean to be at him at some favourable moment. We have warlike accounts from China, but no news since the new Admiral & Plenipo arrived there. Poor Hal's letters are, I fear me, gone to London, & will be stale, when I get them. [Usual family greetings.]

Your ever affectionate son,
Mauger.

LETTER XV

From MAUGER MONK, Mussoorie
To ISABELLA MONK, Ann's Place, Guernsey.
Per Overland Mail via Falmouth.

16 NOVEMBER 1841

My Dearest Bell,

I was going to be very lazy this month, for in good truth I have been much worked of late, & almost threw myself into a fever from the excitement the examination caused me. It was a glorious one; even the proud Scot, I serve, could not contain his satisfaction, so in the fulness of his heart, he allowed it to be the best his scholars had ever passed but now acts as tho' he regretted having given vent to his feelings. But to the motive wh roused me. One of my boxes has just arrived; foils, masks, gloves every thing, safe & untouched. I am now writing with dear Madge's leopard pattern slippers on my feet, & my bearer is decorating a shirt front with three of the buttons & a Europe needle with Europe thread are employed to put them on. The foils are the best I ever handled. Thanks, sincerest thanks to you all. May your shadows never be less & the health of all, particularly that of my dear kind father, improve daily. O'Brien has had two or three severe attacks of illness & been unable to write but I am daily expecting a letter from him with some account of the clothes, wh are not, I trust, being paraded about Calcutta on the back of some strong-smelling heavily-scented gentleman of colour. I have no fears about their safety ...

On the 15th Decr, the commencement of our holidays, I go to Meerut to see what prospects this tremendous canal, wh is to be fed by the united streams of the Ganges & Jumna, may open to me; for another twelve month's schoolmastering will, I think, suffice me for life. Government employ must as I have often, too often perhaps, stated be my first object & I have been dissuaded from entering the Grd Trigonom Survey of India by the great Bahadoor himself, the head of the department, & certainly the most affable, open & gentlemanly man I have had an hour's conversation with in India. My present engagement here terminates on the 31st Oct 1842 & I don't think I shall renew, as I am scraping a few rupees together to cut out something for myself. Do you notice any change coming over me? Egad! I think before many more years are over my head I shall have taken up with Byron's "good old gentlemanly vice, avarice " I hope not, however; but you know I am always in extremes, & never cod hit the "golden mean", the "medio tutissimus" ...

I have felt somewhat ashamed of the hasty letter I wrote Uncle Will last month, but I felt like a schoolboy let loose for a week, went shooting in the Dhoon for that time with every expectation of getting good sport & came back with my friend Wilson, disappointed. The jungles were so thick, & the dogs, used to hill shooting, so wild, that thirty nine head of game, including two beautiful leopards, five spotted deer, & three wild boar, the latter killed in fair fight with spears on horseback, were all that rewarded our six days hard work. The scenery too, after the mountains, was tame in the extreme to my eye so I took but one sketch, the pleasure of spending an hour by the side of a dark-eyed, dusky peasant, being my principal inducement even to do that. I have just got over another love-fit, but am not now quite poz that I liked the young lady so well as certain bits of company's paper & shares in various companies wh she is said to possess. Certain it is that the honour of two days in her company cured me effectually. I could have worn a great coat all the time & really believe she wod freeze a fellow in a dog-day in the tropics. Luckily for me, my blood does not easily stagnate in my veins.

I cannot omit to mention the gratification that I felt on hearing that poor unfortunate Davey's children had not been left wholly destitute, as I imagined they were likely to be. I shall be delighted to hear that Lambe has recovered his senses, & his wife shown more of the woman & less of the lawyer than I fear has hitherto been the case. O'Brien has promised me to shew William every attention in his power when the Himalaya arrives at Calcutta. I have written to him a letter, wh awaits his coming, but cod hold out no prospect to him in the N.W. provinces of Hindostan.

[Usual family greetings.]

LETTER XVI

From MAUGER MONK, Mussoorie
To SARAH MAGRATH, Guernsey.
Endorsed: Guernsey 13 Feb 1842.

15 DECEMBER 1841

My Dearest Sister,

[Disappointed that the last two mails have brought him nothing. However, the missing package via the 'Robarts' is on its way up.]

We have just broken up & I am off for the holidays to Meerut to watch "the coming events", wh have been for some time casting their shadows before, & see if I can carve out any thing under government either for my pen or my sword. With the Afghans in rebellion, Caubul blockaded, our officers butchered & convoys plundered; the Punjaub (Lahore) only waiting a favourable opportunity for an outbreak; the Sikhs & Chinese fighting it out in Little Thibet; the Nepalese invading our Eastern frontier at the instigation of China; & the Kingdom of Oude divided against itself (all wh things are without exaggeration calling the attention of government at the present moment) a jolly adventurer, for I can call myself nothing better, may find good & profitable employment. I wish they wd give me command of one of the mountain passes, all by the bye now unguarded. We have lost some 60 or 70 officers in Afghanistaun alone within the last three months, Sir Alexr Burnes, the British envoy & his brother among the number.

The winter here has set in early & promises to be very severe. The snow, wh has fallen very heavily, wod, independent of other circumstances, have been sufficient to prevent my taking a trip into the interior as I originally intended. My grey head, however, reminds me that it is pretty nigh time I was settling myself in some permanent employment; but I believe the Lord only knows when the rolling stone will stop & begin to allow the moss to gather. When this happens I shall begin to talk to you about yr youngsters (God bless them & you kiss them all round for me). How do [you] like your new house? I know but of one drawback, & that is the view of the roadstead & castle, the loss of wh the old granite house & iron railings of your neighbour Mr. Lefebvre will certainly not repay; but then you have a nice garden & are not so much entertained, as you were in the Pollet, with the infernal noise of the carts.

I am well assured that you left the old house with regret. I sometimes whisper a wish to myself that I cod spend even a month with you in Guernsey, & then return but I fear that the day, wh is to see me in Guernsey is far distant. Without a moderate fortune I shall never return; for I am totally unfitted for any home-employment, & am too fond of the wide range of the jungle to settle in any place so circumscribed as I shod feel the dear little isle to be, particularly where game is not. As much about yourselves & the island in yr next, my dear Sarah; for I never tire on that subject. A letter from home keeps the steam up & yr brother as lively as a young colt for a fortnight together, & if followed by a good day's sport, as it generally is, adds another week to his high spirits, wh the prospect of an epistle by the succeeding mail does not allow to flag. A merry Xmas & a happy new year to you all. I know you won't forget those over the water, & I promise to toss off a bumper "to those whom we love at home'. All health & prosperity surround you. Commend me with all fraternal affection, aye &

kisses, if you like, tho' by this time they are nothing new to him, to Nicholas & the girls. Good husbands to them too. My prayers are ever for the comfort & happiness of our dear father, to whom my sincerest love & regards ...

The Imperial Chateau was built on a spur above the Library by HH Jajatjit Singh, the Maharajah of Kapurthala

LETTER XVII

From MAUGER MONK, Mussoorie

To HUGH MONK.

[Endorsements: as 37, plus]: "Landour 14 Feb 1842. Paid 6 Ans."

"Guernsey Apr 14 1842" "Answered April 25 1842"

14 FEBRUARY 1842

My Dearest Father,

I regretted much to find by your letter of the 2nd Novr that you were suffering from complaints, which, tho' likely not to prove serious in their effects, were sufficient to debar you from the comforts necessary to you in your declining years; I mean books and exercise; & sincerely hope with yourself that the tumour on your ribs may not prove of consequence. The letter was awaiting my return from my customary trip during the vacation, & which on this occasion combined business & sporting (my only amusement), to which latter I am by chance indebted for making the acquaintance of a gentn of the Civil Service, whom I may hereafter find a friend. The result of my observations are these: That as Classical Assistant here, I hold a station equal to the highest of the government clerks in point of rank, & that a recommendation from my present employer would in itself be a sufficient guarantee of my ability, integrity & moral character. 2ndly that by accepting any mercantile situation (two were offered me while at Meerut with high salaries) I should be placing myself in the hands of men, who are trading on the capital of others, &

not, as it appeared to me, of much principal or----ple, spell it which way you please, both will answer the description best. Besides, however lucrative, my station would be somewhat lower than it is at present & as money was never my deity, I think health with a competence in the hills is not to be put in the balance against wealth with a broken constitution in the plains. The times too are out of joint: everything seemed while I was at Meerut & Delhi to be in a whirl of uncertainty & confusion. I left the former place on the 13th, & saw scarce a Xtian face till I reached my home on the 28th ulto. There I found that one of my subordinates had resigned to gratify an appetite for mountain ranging & pass exploring, & a second poor fellow, of the name of MacLachlan, whom I believe I mentd in one of my former letters to you, had died suddenly of a rupture of the heart a few days before. Assistants are of course not readily to be procured here, so the burden of the work has fallen on the principal & myself for the present. There too I heard for the first time of the insurrection of the Afghan chiefs in Caubul, or rather of its termination, one of the most melancholy that ever befel the British arms in any quarter of the world. The particulars will reach Engd as soon as this, so I will now only give you the last act of the series of political blunders committed by that most unenergetic of Governors General, Lord Auckland, & his envoy, Sir Wm. MacNachten.

Notwithstanding the well-known treachery of the Afghans, Sir Wm. M attended only by 4 officers went to a conference with Mahomed Achtan, the son of Dost Mahomed, the deposed Ameer of Caubul, & was for his folly together with a Captn Trevor of the Cavalry shot during the conference by Mahomed Achtar himself, the other three officers being made prisoners. His second in command, Major Eldred Pottinger, thought himself bound to carry thro' the treaty commenced by the murdered envoy, & as he was the political, directed poor old Genl Elphinstone to evacuate Caubul forthwith, & this in the very depth of winter. The assassination of Sir Wm. had not opened their eyes; & the consequences of this last piece of imprudence was the murder of nearly the whole army 5500 strong, one only, a Dr. Brydon having reached Jellalabad, wounded in nine places, to tell the tale. The sepoys from cold & exhaustion were unable to fight, the greater part were slaughtered, & those, who were made prisoner, have been sold as slaves at a rupee a head to the Oosbegs. Coll Anquetil, a Jerseyman I believe, has with his own regt, H. M.'s 44th, perished. Of that corps, 700 strong & Captain Nicholls' troop of Horse Arty (6 guns) not one man or officer remains alive. They fought to the last. One lady out of the 35 or 40, who accompanied the troops on their retreat, was killed by her husband's side, & he himself shortly after shot, while defending his mother-in-law, Lady Sale, who is also desperately wounded. The remg ladies with the few surviving officers are detained as hostages till the final evacuation of Afghanistaun.

I received the letter that the post office had detained dated Apr 28 1840 at Chusan but have since recd another from Henry dated Amoy, Sept 2 1841. Of the four he has written me these two have only come to hand. He states in his last that he had written to Bell five weeks & to you ten days before. I despatched an answer to him the day before yesterday & failed not to comply with your wishes. He appears to enjoy excellent health & spirits & seems not a little proud of having been in medical charge of the Marine Battn during their eight days Campaign at Canton. I shall write to Aunt Wm & Bell next month, & to William as soon as I can get rid of a tormenting headache I have had for the last week, owing to my partaking of the excitement of the times & being rather over-worked. The massacred troop of HA at Caubul was the one I belonged to previous to my being transferred to the Foot as Battn writer. I am also very much afraid I have fallen in love but am not quite certain. I have got medicine by me but don't like to take it, being liable to exposure & draught & the weather piercingly cold. With kindest love & kisses to my dearest sisters & all affection to my Uncles & Aunts; & with sincerest prayers for your restoration to health, I remain, my dearest Father,

Your most affectionate & dutiful son,
Mauger.

P.S. Both boxes have arrived safe. I did not write last month to any one.

LETTER XVIII

From MAUGER MONK, Mussoorie

To ISABELLA MONK, Ann's Place, Guernsey.

[Endorsement:] "The correspondence of Miss Monk [deleted] with her beloved brother before joined in the holy & delightful liason herein mentioned."

12 APRIL 1842

Bell,

My own darling, tho' I've nothing of interest to communicate, I can't allow this mail to go without thanking you for your delightful January epistle. Egad! I almost think from your style that for lack of occupation you are about to turn authoress & mount les bas bleux, an ugly chaussure, tho' I, en passant, to set off your foot & ankle. Your bits of home news are quite delicious; they set me scheming & thinking of by-gone days, containing too many happy scenes to let the others of less pleasant nature affect my spirits, which do, however, like the funds, vacillate a great deal & occasionally get very low—particularly this season, during which I have been & am still likely to be worked more than ever: for no qualified persons have been found to replace my two unfortunate juniors, who died last year. My friend, Wilson, is in Thibet, or exploring the passes and I have not a single companion to have an hour's chat with over a quiet glass of punch in the evening; nor do I ever go out now, having found it necessary to part with my favourite, Caubulee (horse), who, becoming more religiously disposed than I approved of was sold at considerably less than half of what he cost me. I don't mind an occasional roll when on the plains, but am decidedly of the opinion that the horse, which from time to time evinces a disposition to drop on his knees in the hills cannot be pronounced other than highly dangerous. Besides him who sits in 'the high places' & myself, there are at present but two assistants, the writing master & his son, (a darkey) who takes charge of the juveniles. With the former I found it absolutely necessary to take the first favourable opportunity of quarrelling; for, my dear Bell, he has a daughter, the loveliest & most amiable girl of colour I have seen in the country. Her descent by the father's side is Jewish, evident enough in the contour of her beautiful face & in her eye.

Now it happens that your susceptible brother might possibly have thrown himself in one of his spooney fits into the young lady's arms, had not interest stepped in & cooly told him: Your prospects will be d----d if you do. Love & interest had a long argument, I assure you: & while, the latter had the upper hand, she adroitly took great offence at something that was said by the young lady's father & kicked up a row, which ended in a complete break; & as is the custom of the country, all the family followed in the wake of the head thereof, who, like all renegades, is one of those canting hypocrites, who bandy about the Almighty's name, when conversing on the most ordinary topics. Even now my passion has much to struggle with; for, living as we do, under the same roof, it is not always possible to avoid meeting. Each of her eyes is a piercer. Had I not the most utter contempt for & detestation of her parent, I am afraid it would be all up with me, in spite of the Eastern blood that runs in her veins. The prejudices of Europeans in that respect have not yet infected me. So much for love. I can readily dispose of the two or three dozen young ladies that are ready for exportation carriage paid & insured against loss of charms, they would turn out a very profitable speculation if you could get anyone to advance the funds. All, as you say, being very pretty, I will guarantee their being disposed of in six months, pledging myself to retain all who may remain on hand at the end of that time after their arrival. With one at each of my favourite shooting stations I could very well manage half a dozen myself. It wouldn't do to keep them all together. The advancer of the funds, being in for a good spec might perhaps be induced to take a lot of juvenile brownies in exchange warranted sound & with excellent appetites. If there be any one, who is anxious to make the most of his loose cash, I have not the slightest objection to borrow from £500 to £1000 on personal security at 5 per cent. I can always make 12 per cent of it up here, & generally more, but would be very well contented to put the odd seven in my own pocket.

Evening. Apr: 13 1842

Having no one else to talk to or anything else to speak about yesterday evening, I gave you a fuller story of self & self's weaknesses than I intended, tho' I feel a strong inclination to tear up what I have written, I am afraid it would only be to give you another batch of nonsense. We are all on the tiptoe of expectation to hear of the forcing of the Khyber Pass, leading to Afghanistan, which was to have taken place on the lst—the primary object of the large force, now marching into that country under Genl. Pollock, being to release Sir Robt Sale & H.M.'s 13th Lt. Infantry, who have been blockaded there for some months, in Jallalabad, whose provisions will only last to the 7th: & then to wreak unsparing vengeance on the Afghans for their damnable treachery, that is, if they will stop to fight.

H.M.'s 44th, who had been brutally used by their Commn Coll Shelton, refused to fight on their retreat from Cabool & were cut down to a man without resistance, feeling a sullen satisfaction in perishing themselves on seeing their officers slaughtered with them. The remains of the H.A, after spiking their guns, cut the traces of their horses & with Captn Nicholls at their head rushed into the midst of the enemy's horse, where all met at least an honourable death, no quarter being asked or given. One regiment, the 37th Native followed their example & were cut off to a man without stirring from the position they had taken up, & surrounded by numbers of the fallen enemy. Old dare devil Genl. Nott has recently beaten off an immense force, which was besieging him in Candahar, with only four native regiments, a few irregular Cavalry & a company of Foot Arty, all pretty nigh half starved, & strange to say, without the loss of a single man.

I hope Hal will be able to knock out a few dollars as his share of the China prize money. Poor fellow! He will need some to make good his loss. Having heard from him about Xmas, I do not look forward to another letter till June or July. He seemed quite pleased at having been put in medical charge of the Marine Battalion. The Chinamen appear to be bad shots, a hole in a sub's shoulder, some trifling wound among the men, and a perforation in some naval officer's glazed cocked hat (an excellent target by the bye) being the amount of one morning's damage.

While at Meerut during the holidays, an old lady of the name of Ross, formerly a Miss Jennings of the High St, hearing that I was a Guernseyman, requested me by a mutual friend to call upon her. She entertained me most hospitably, & tho' forty-seven years in India and sixty-seven in age still bears the marks of her juvenile beauty, for which it appears she was once remarkable. Her faculties too, altho' a martyr to rheumatism, are entirely unimpaired, & there is not perhaps a more businesslike, cheerful & at the same time, really devout woman in the country. With grown up & [?] intelligent sons about her, she allows none of them to meddle with her affairs; yet they seldom fail to consult her on any important [point?] of their own. Seeing that she completely gloated over the little views you sent me in your letters, I gave them to her & have promised when a parcel is coming out to me to ask my dear sister for one of the sets for her [... ...] mind when sending this way to let me have one for her, & you may include one for myself. As she is a lady of no small influence, if you will send them by post, I don't mind the expense, for I should like to gratify her, intending to do myself the honour of a visit next Xmas. Adieu, my dearest Bell, I am looking forward to the end of the month for Papa's promised letter. Give my kindest love to Aunt & Uncle Bill, Aunt Eliza & Uncle James, & remember me to all whom you think I should like to be mentioned to or who deign to make any enquiries, & with every sincere feeling of love & affection to our dear Father, Sarah & her, I trust, happy household, my dolce far niente sister Madge, believe me to remain ever

Your devotedly fond brother,
Mauger.

Apr. 15. 12 Noon.

News just come in. The Khyber forced after a desperate resistance. Loss heavy, particularly in H.M.'s 9th (the Holy Boys). Afghans & [?] lying dead in heaps. Seik Auxiliaries from Lahore behaved nobly.

LETTER XIX

From MAUGER MONK, Mussoorie

To HUGH MONK, Guernsey.

Endorsements as 37, plus]: "India. Landour May 8 Pd 6 Ans" "Guernsey Jy 10 1842" "Answered July 25th including a Letter of Credit on Messrs Cockerell & Co from Messrs Drummonds, London for £500" Seal bears Hugh Monk's griffin crest.

8 MAY 1842

My Dearest Father,

The letter from you, which Bell had led me to expect in April, was delayed, I deeply regretted to find from Sarah's letter, by your eyes being again afflicted with the old complaint, to you, I know from your habits, doubly painful & inconvenient, debarring you, as it, must, from your customary enjoyments of outdoor exercise & reading. The latter I feel well assured my dear sisters would find a substitute for, by reading to you themselves; tho', until rendered so by habit listening is not quite so agreeable as ocular perusal.

The schoolmaster's collar being now pretty well adjusted, I seldom make any attempt to kick over the traces, and as even the monotony of my present calling has from inducing habits of the strictest regularity, become rather pleasant than otherwise, I have of late amused my evenings (for I am without a companion) by dispassionately comparing my situation with that of the uncovenanted employees of the H.C.'s service, & find the balance inclining to my own side, as thus: In point of respectability, termed precedence here, I yield to none save the Deputy Collectors; & tho' my present salary be inferior only to servants of long standing & known worth in nominal amount; divest theirs of the travelling expenses, tentage & camel hire, to which they are subjected three or four times a year, & the real amounts will not vary much. In the year I believe I should find myself the gainer. Food is certainly cheaper in the plains, servant's wages more moderate; but they must pay for their own medical attendance. Were not my own active & sportsmanlike habits with the bracing air of the mountains, under the blessing of Providence my best physician, I am guaranteed the surgeon's care by my agreement. An occasional brace of pheasants or partridges to the doctor keeps us on excellent terms, & he seldom meets me without a joke on my having never been under his hands. God knows what sort of a surgeon he may be, but when a man, high in his profession too in the H.C.'s service, asserts sulphate and sulphurate of potass to be one & the same thing, one cannot but entertain very rational doubts as to his intimate acquaintance with chemistry. Excuse the digression; add to what I have already said, the disgusting way in which they are reprimanded, & trampled on by their superiors, & to which being mostly country-born they submit with a sort of "God is great" patience;- and the mere pittance, which is allowed them to keep body & soul together after thirty years service, and you will, I think, agree with me that I may go further & fare much worse. Few ever obtain the pension, trifling as it is, that I have mentioned, exposure & climate have in most cases done their worst, ere the happy hour of retirement arrives. Tis true that by Mackinnon's death I should be thrown out of employ; but quaere, would it not be into a better? Ours is the only school for boys in the hills, & my having been any time in the employ of so strict and feared (more feared I believe than respected) a man as Mackinnon, would be worth a host of other recommendations.

The object of this comparison, I almost hear you say, tis thus; that being about to renew my engagement for a term on favourable terms, I want your [a word missing here?] and if it can be granted without any inconvenience to yourself & the other members of the family, in establishing myself as member of the community, on being able to take part in the common interests of the station, which is to be in future my home, as it has been for the last three years. Mr. Bohle, Mackinnon's father-in-law, is fast drawing to his end, & want of education & skill in conducting his affairs has so involved him, that to the hammer his estates must go. The one he possesses here is worth about 10,000 Rupees, & is eligibly situated. Less than half that sum will probably purchase it, & I need hardly say, that in contemplating it & its advantages I have broken the tenth commandment. If, then, it can be done without detriment to your income, I would ask of my dear father the loan of £500 for 7 years at a clear interest of 5 percent per annum, all discount & diff in rate of exchange to be defrayed by me. Security for the capital would be given by registering the estate in our joint names "or the survivor of them", thereby vesting the estate in you, should I die. Its improvement being my constant care, it would, I doubt not, realise the amount borrowed on a resale. A collateral bond, or judgment in ouster with power of sale by you alone on non-payment of principal at the time specified would secure the repayment of the money advanced at the proper time. Estates here have no title deeds;- all are registered at the District Judges & tranfers can only be made by the parties in whose names they stand, or in their representatives, if deceased. Almost secure of 12 per cent I should have offered a higher rate of interest, which would only had led you to believe that I had a mare's nest in view, & prevented probably in the outset any consideration of my proposal. Should you entertain it favourably, a letter from your London agents stating the amount placed at my disposal by you & empowering me to draw at sight or short dates would enable me by sale of bills to that amount to the "Agra" Bank to realise almost half a year's interest being the period during which this money might be lying unproductive. The moral influence I should then possess would be of no mean assistance in forming an advantageous matrimonial alliance, to which I am, in good sooth, not at all disinclined. I trust you will not, my dearest Father, consider this as a begging letter, but rather as a statement setting forth certainly my advantage & advancement, without detriment either to yourself or my brothers & sisters. I cannot spin out my letter more now. From China I do not look to hear till June or July & I believe I gave you enough of Afghan politics in my last. Matters are going on better now. To Sarah, whose welcome letter I recd last month, Magrath & their lovely bairns, my dearest Bell & Madge my most fraternal love & kisses. Heaven keep you in health & bless you is the sincere prayer of

Your dutiful & affectionate son,
Mauger.

P.S. The retrospect of my past life in which I indulged on my birthday, the 5th inst sent me to bed a wiser but not a happier man.

LETTER XX

From MAUGER MONK, Mussoorie
To SARAH MAGRATH, Guernsey.

1 JULY 1842

Sarah, My dearest Sister,

Never let your conscience trouble you about leaving me without a letter for some time. Write only when your maternal and apothecarial cares will allow you, & believe that your affectionate brother regrets that his occupations will not allow of his transmitting home a monthly budget of letters. My best thanks for your last and its interesting contents, in return for which I would fain give you something amusing at least, but have neither matter at the moment, nor am I particularly "in the vein". You might derive some entertainment were I to give you some of my fanciful flights. Heavens! What a mass of ruins are the many Chateaux d'Espagne which some of my solitary evenings have constructed, to be dispelled, alas! Like the mists of a Bengal morning, by the rising sun, leaving no wreck behind. And, if the Spanish proverb be true, my "good intentions" have added to hell's pavement a splendid specimen of Mosaic.

The mail, which arrived in June, brot me a most cheering letter from our dear old Father. He speaks of his ailments as on the decline, and writes not only in apparently excellent spirits, but (in addition to much good advice on the subject) even jocosely respecting matrimony. He points to your little community as a condition to which I may expect to come. Heaven bless the bairns! I could almost wish myself a dozen such. Malgré tout le conseil que j'ai reçu from all hands, I am fairly enamoured of matrimony, but who is to have the honour of being my lady-wife Heaven only knows. I've been two years on the look out, and can find none of the fair sex within a moderate distance of my standard. Now don't call me vain, for, sister dear, its a very moderate one. Be not, however, surprised some fine day at my introducing by letter a fresh member of the family, but take my word she will be worthy of admission.

My life continues the same monotonous round—hard work during 101/2 months of the year, and six weeks unrestrained indulgence, principally in visiting different stations and my favourite pastime of shooting. Hospitality is the chief trait in the character of the Anglo Indian, and amongst the mercantile community, where most of my few acquaintances are, the good things of this life are ungrudgingly and abundantly supplied. My term of engagement ends in October and will be renewed, with an increase of salary and other advantages not yet definitely settled, nor as far as I am concerned likely to be so till Septr. I have seen enough, of late, and during my last trip to the plains not to put myself under any of the H.C.'s Civil Servants—the most insulting bullies to their subordinates it is possible to conceive. Besides, the benefit of a larger salary would be swallowed up in the necessary expences of travelling, and that too at all seasons of the year, without any allowed period of relaxation. Here I know what time I can call my own, and dispose of it according to my own pleasure. This station, too, is so healthy that I would sacrifice a much larger salary to remain where I am, provided I had a nice little wife to keep me company; and one I will have before I am a year older. I care little about society, but "Oh! Solitude, where are the charms etc". I see by my dear Bell's letters that half the world at home are marrying and giving in marriage, and sincerely do I wish my charming sisters could find worthy suitors on whom to bestow themselves Bell in particular, as she seems to be making up her mind to celibacy and a pet cat. I would fain send them something worth their acceptance and the carriage home, but we mountaineers are a homely race, wearing for the most part home spun cloth and wanting but little. At Delhi I could have purchased many nice nic nacs, inferior in workmanship to those of Europe and equally, if not more expensive; and now that I have damaged skins enough of the golden pheasant to make a couple of feather tippets, I can get no tailor in these desolate regions to come and work under my superintendence; and I might just as well give them away as trust them out of my sight. However, I have a few trifles for Aunt William to send off in October after the rains, and shall send them the skins then, if nothing more. I cannot write to Papa this month, but acknowledge for me with many, very many thanks, the receipt of his letter, and as he is anxious to know my whereabouts he may hit it to a nicety on a large map of India in Long.78° 3′ 15″ East and Lat.30° 28′ 29″ N. almost due north of Saharunpore. I must now bring my letter to a close and write to my dear Aunt at Clapton but pray excuse the long list of friends to be kindly remembered to. I give you Carte blanche to distribute them without limit and confine myself to our immediate circle ... [Usual family greetings.] ... believe me to remain, ever

Your attached and loving brother
M. Fitzh. Monk.

P.S. I'm on the look out daily for a letter from Hal. Sir H. Gough and the Admiral have been at it hammer and tongs with but very trifling loss to the barbarians, and the devil to pay among the Celestials.

LETTER XXI

A note in HUGH MONK's hand.

25 JULY 1842 [?]

On 25th July a letter was forwarded to him [Mauger] viâ Falmouth containing a letter of credit to the House of Messrs Cockerell and Co of Calcutta in his favour for £500 and also containing a Bank of England Power of Attorney, which he is desired to execute & return without delaying.

LETTER XXII

From MAUGER MONK, Mussoorie

To HUGH MONK, Guernsey.

[Endorsements as 37, plus]: "Answered October 23rd 1842."

9 AUGUST 1842

My Dearest Father,

How welcome was your last letter; how glad was I to find by its length & clearness that the complaint in your eyes had been removed & how much more have I to be thankful to you, when you have made scruple about stating that writing is to you now a serious undertaking. I thought that I had been pretty full in my accounts of the "seminary" & its "principal", with whom I have perhaps kept on better terms than I should otherwise have done, from the total absence of all curiosity on my part into any thing not immediately connected with my own duties; so much so, indeed, that altho' I have been with him the best part of three years I never yet saw the scholars at table, nor entered the schoolroom even whilst the tables were laying. No; Mackinnon is a Highlander with a strong, comprehensive mind, a full share of the common sense of his country, but obstinate & unwilling to accept aid, for which he has not agreed to give an equivalent. To offer a suggestion unasked is to insult him. It jars on his 'independence of mind' & perhaps clashes with the principles by which he is guided. To differ with him on any point he may ask your opinion on is to provoke a discussion which terminates in a decided coldness on his part, which he, in general, wants frankness to remove. During the first year I was with him he took a sulky fit at my not pronouncing "Rome" Room & requested me to be guided in my Latin by the "Grad-dus" as he termed it.

A visit from the bishop a few months after settled the matter;- for with true Guernsey stubbornness I persisted. Room was corrected on all occasions by the Right Reverend Father & his chaplain, & the pure English enunciation of Latin in the classes under my charge quietly commanded. I cautiously shewed no exultation, nor ever alluded to the subject, but found shortly after that my boys had strict orders to attend to every thing I told them. Still it was not till about three months ago, that he had the frankness to thank me for my "obstinacy" & then laughingly told me that tho' his ear was now attuned to Anglo-Latin, it was not & never would be to Anglo-Greek, freely avowing at the same time my equality in knowledge of that language, & thanking me before the scholars for the assistance I had given his own class, whenever he had been absent. At present we are more friendly than we ever were, but do not visit. He sends me papers & periodicals & I occasional presents of game to him. It cost me some time & study to know him, but I do so now. He understands me too thoroughly, tho', I think, he for a long time believed my natural frankness to be assumed as a cover to latent objects.

From various causes I have acquired some habits of eccentricity which may perhaps appear in correspondence, & from want of society feel that all my letters must be very egotistical. I try to correct the inclination to be so as much as I can, but monotony & solitude have made the habit strong. My engagement terminates on the 31st Oct but no application for its renewal shall ever be made by me. If he wishes me to remain, he must ask me, for I have two situations, into either of which I can walk on the lst Nov. & a recently received letter from Major Genl Smith, to which I have returned a respectful answer, states, that 'if Mr. Monk would point out any thing in which he is of opinion any service could be rendered, a ready & willing consideration would be given to the request.' He has nothing better to bestow than I hold at present, & in those military offices all that a person can save in quarters, is swallowed up when the Commander-in-Chief & his camp are in motion. In my reply I have left myself open to avail myself of his patronage should circumstances call for it, at any time, & begged him to convey my most grateful thanks to the generous friend, to whom I am indebted for the honour of his notice. Be kind enough to do the same for me & let Mrs. Sargent know that I feel grateful for her kindness. I must now reserve what more I have to say on the subject of the school & my hopes & prospects for another letter. Next month or the following one will have decided me one way or another.

Harry's last letter (date, Marine Qrs, Chusan, Apr: 25) is an excellent one. He still continues doing duty with the Marine Battalion, of which he is in medical charge. At the battle of Tsekee he was Senior Medical Officer with Captn Bourchier's detachment of Sailors & Marines. He was mentioned in Adml Parker's letter to the Admiralty, published by Government in the Indian papers, as having been present; but of all these things he tells me he has sent home accounts of the same date as mine or thereabouts. Many thanks for your cautions when out hunting. I am seldom rash, tho' dotingly fond of the sport. Tell my dear Bell, to whom & Madge all love & kisses, that I must plead my onerous duties as an excuse for not writing by this mail. With regard to Afghanistan we receive news three days earlier than they do at Delhi, the nearest city.

Your hints upon marriage shall not be lost upon me but if I remain, a wife I must have, & that before the lst Feb next, when the school reopens after the Xmas vacation. Kindest love to Sarah

& Magrath, & say all you please to amuse their dear little bairns, Heaven's blessings on their heads. My kindest regards to my Uncles & Aunts both in Glatney & Clapton & commendations to all inquiring friends. God bless you with health & keep you yet many years is the sincere prayer of

Your affectionate son,
M. Fitzh. Monk.

LETTER XXIII

From MAUGER MONK, Mussoorie

To ISABELLA MONK, Ann's Place, Guernsey.

Per Overland Mail, viâ Falmouth.

SEPTEMBER 1842

My Dearest Isabella,

You really bring a charge against me, to which I cannot possibly plead guilty. Sweetly unconscious am I of ever having grumbled or found fault with your ever welcome epistles, nor will my wretched memory assist me in recalling to mind what I may have written a fortnight after my letters are dispatched the contents of each letter are completely obliterated from my recollection. It is not so, however, with those I receive from home. They remain deeply impressed. The evidences of my delinquency are in your hands; & freely do I confess you are a most lenient judge. Let me therefore promise to their less "crankiness" in future for if I offer you as well as my dear Aunt whose forgiveness I have asked, Je serai bien au désespoir.

I cannot thank you better for the views of the island received together with your last letter, which I conclude you shortened as a punishment for my alleged quiz than by quoting the reply of my friend & towney "Mrs. Ross". "Your kind favour reached me in due time & afforded me very great pleasure. I am much indebted to your friendly attention. The views you have so obligingly sent me are really beautiful. St. Peter's Port is exquisite. How well do

I remember many a spot represented in it & how dear to me are the recollections of many places in the island," after, as she states in another part of her letter, an absence of "more than forty-seven years." Her first husband's name was "Voisey". The old lady, who by the bye is a martyr to rheumatism, a complaint in this country of a most painful character, tho' too general to meet with much sympathy, speaks, as do the remnants of the old 8th Drag[oon]s or "the King's Royal Irish", as they prefer to be called, in the highest terms of poor old "Uncle John", his attention & kindness to the men, his benevolence to the distressed, & what I certainly never heard remarked upon at home, his great skill as a medical practitioner. They praise his bravery & coolness when obliged to discharge his duties under a heavy fire:- particularly at Hattrass; & they scruple not to laugh immoderately at his peculiarities, his style of equitation & the tricks which used to be played on him by the regimental scamps. An introduction to any of the few survivors of that regiment, who are all comfortably settled & well to do in the world in about Meerut & Cawnpore, as "old Snicks's [?] nephew" never fails to ensure me a most hearty reception, & on more than one occasion, when I mentioned his death, I have seen the honest tribute of a tear stealing down the cheek of a furrowed veteran, followed by an anecdote commemorative of the old doctor's kindness in some particular instance to the payer. I have thought it a circumstance worthy of remark that with the character of recklessness & daring which the 8th bore in India, I have become acquainted with no individual belonging to it, or rather, who once belonged to it, that was not of a serious turn of mind, & highly respected by the community.

Now, my dearest sister, don't misinterpret what you may be pleased to term the love passages in my letters. I never told you, to my recollection, that I had been seriously in love, nor did I ever hazard the falsehood of stating that I had proposed

& been rejected. That I have been long seeking a wife, I frankly avow, & quite as frankly assure you that I would rather remain single & lonely all my days than take as the partner of my bosom any of the listless, formal, dawdling, one-idead, tho' certainly many of them, very pretty, creatures, with whom I have become acquainted. As to being refused, believe me, I run scarcely any risk of that; for let my personal & mental qualifications be what they may, I trust, you will scarce class me among the brutes. I enjoy a salary & perquisites which none of the young & few of the elderly men in the N.W. Provinces receive. I mean of course those who are not the Honble Comps[?] covenanted servants. In a country where marriages are often contracted without the parties seeing each other, salary & age are the two things first ascertained. You may one day hear of my being married, but as to much of what I understand by the word "love" entering the matter, I consider quite another thing. The little God will find my armour of worldly mindedness proof against his shafts, did he aim them at me, whom, from his dislike of grey heads, he will probably let alone. I can give you an instance of the coolness with which I consider these matters; so call me "apathetic" if you like. Resolution I certainly do not want. On one young lady alone, the daughter of a near neighbour, did I ever bestow a serious thought & I was induced to it more by her sound common sense and affectionate disposition than any personal attractions, which however she does not want, being the most beautiful girl of colour I have seen in this [?] country. I was much struck with her at first, nor upon longer acquaintance, now almost a year, has my opinion altered or my esteem diminished, but, disgusted with her old father's never ceasing cant & twaddle, & seeing the possibility of having a young sister, whom the fool of a father has spoilt & whom I detest, thrown on my hands in the event of his death, & perhaps having an Anglo-Indian antipathy to the small portion of a warmer blood which flows in her veins, (her mother was a half-caste & she is very fair) I found no difficulty in restraining myself within the bounds of simple friendship. I may add without vanity, that I have no difficulty in perceiving that my company is much more agréable than that of the rest of her acquaintances.

I must now change the topic tho' I be still the subject. In my last month's letter to my dear father I mentioned an intention of making no application to Mr. Mackinnon about a fresh engagement but an offer to conduct a branch of a mercantile establishment & Major Genl Smith's kindly volunteering to exert his patronage, which however is but small, in my behalf, "could I point out any thing in which any services could be [… …] I rendered", I wrote to Mr. M requesting him to inform me if the discharge of my duties & my general deportment had been so far to his satisfaction as to ensure me a fresh engagement, to which I received the following reply: "My Dear Mr. Monk, There could in justice to you, be but one answer to your note just received; and I lose no time in assuring you that I have had every reason to be fully satisfied with the manner in which you have discharged your duties, and deported yourself generally, since you have been with me. If you had good prospects elsewhere, I should have great pleasure in formally certifying your character and talents, in such a way, as, I have no doubt, would recommend you strongly to the head of a public office; but, if I am to understand by your note, that you would like to remain in your present situation, I shall be very happy to enter into a fresh engagement with you. Yours sincerely, I. Mackinnon. 20 Augt 1842. "As I knew I had discharged my duty faithfully, I looked but for terms of general approbation and was so surprised at this unexpected answer, coming from a man, not given to encomium, & who requires the strict fulfilment of his bond, that I believe I dropped a tear or two of real satisfaction. Of this, however, I will not be certain, for my eyes felt so dim and watery at the moment that I could not clearly see what fell. I have many reasons for preferring to remain here to entering the public service, but with the exception of a superior climate on one side, and the insulting manner in which many public officials treat their subordinates on the other, & these in themselves are reasons sufficient, you must be content for the present that I keep my motives for such preference to myself. The terms will, I know, be liberal, for of this much I have been assured; but Mackinnon has requested me to delay the conclusion of the agreement a week or two longer, to which I have consented, the more readily as I know him to be a man of honour & as he has been convinced that the stigma attempted to be cast on my character, to which I alluded in a former letter to Papa, viz. that of having purchased a comrade's wife while I was in the artillery, is a malicious falsehood.

Two of my maligners I have found out—the one, who I provided for when starving, is in his grave, which I am not uncharitable enough to wish defiled; for he died miserably last year in my arms, asking pardon of Heaven & me, for what offence I knew not then. The other a despicable dandy, I had the pleasure of horse-whipping round his employer's encampment, which I came unexpectedly upon, whilst enjoying the sports of the chase (my sole delight) a few months since. The fool asked satisfaction, & in my excitement tendered him the choice of my double-barrels, or, as I believe him to be coward, offered him my rifle reserving a double for myself.

"Gentlemen," it appeared, "never settled matters in this way"; & so I summoned my Shikaree from whose cummerbund (waist-cloth) most ominously protruded the butts of Papa's present. As I went to the door of the tent one side, for my Shikaree, carrying two spears & a matchlock could not conveniently enter, out bolted "dishy buck" thro' the other, & I have never seen him since. Nothing but his inordinate vanity can, I understand, bear him up against the jeers of his fellow scribes, to whom I left a fine buck as a present; for the morning was too fine & the game too abundant to accept of their invitation to breakfast.

As I must now bring this to a conclusion or it will be illegible, forget not to return my most grateful acknowledgement to Mrs. Sargent for her kind introduction to the Major-General's notice. I hope this month to receive Aunt Wm's forgiveness & to despatch her birds next month. Your box of the few pretty things I have been able to collect will follow shortly after, as soon as the feather tippets, which take six weeks to make (each) are completed. All love & happiness to Nichs & Sarah, but I have been too unsuccessful in my birds to send him any this season. Next year he shall have a complete set of game birds of the Himalaya. By the bye. If I get spliced I must take the wife to the jungles with me during the holidays; & if I go there unmarried, all matrimonial thoughts will be strangers to me for a month at least. Adieu. With kindest love to my Uncles & Aunts & all sorts of kisses to Sarah's bairns & sincerest prayers for the happiness & health of yourself, my dear Madge & my dearest Father. I am

Your ever fondly attached brother
Mauger.

P.S. Excuse the grease. I've just been trimming my lamp & [?] my fingers.

LETTER XXIV

From MAUGER MONK, Mussoorie
To NICHOLAS MAGRATH, Carrefour, Guernsey.
Endorsed: Guernsey 11 Dec 1842.

15 OCTOBER 1842

My Dear Magrath,

Our dear father, ever too ready to assist our views & advance us in life, has with your aid remitted me a letter of credit on Messrs Cockerell & Co of Calcutta for £500, the receipt of which sum from them I cannot as yet acknowledge for it requires a period of twenty-five days from the time of writing before we can receive an answer from Calcutta, and Papa's letter with its welcome, tho' unexpected enclosures, (for even I had some doubts of the reasonableness of my request for a loan,) only reached me on the evening of the 24th ulto. For the readiness with which you have come forward, accept my best thanks, and in delivering the enclosed power of attorney to my dear father to enable him to repay you give him my most unqualified assurance that I have no other object in view than to lay it out either in government or on real security in this place where I have now, I trust, finally pitched my tent, & where money makes money much faster than it can in England. The amount remitted me shall remain in the Agra Bank at 6 per cent, till a favourable opportunity occurs of laying it out here on an eligible estate. Some are already in the market, consequent on the departure of their owners for Europe,

& more will shortly be so, to defray expences wh this ruinous war in Afghanistan has forced their owners to incur. This war, you will be glad to hear, has come to an end. Ghuznee & Caubul have been retaken, & the former destroyed; & the release of all our prisoners, save one, effected.

To matters of pure speculation I devote nothing but my pen or personal services; & being blessed with tolerable abilities, & this my father's bounty, with an excellent education, which I have not neglected to improve, find that they produce an excellent return without incurring the risk of pecuniary loss. A few weeks back I insured my life for Rs 5000 & doubtless you will ask, with what object? Why, strange to say, that in less than forty-eight hours after I had assured Bell of my stoical indifference to one, to whom I have long been deeply attached, I found myself pouring out to her a longer tale of love & ardent affection than I ever believed my unromantic soul capable of conceiving: in short, I proposed & was accepted, & wod probably ere this, so eloquent has the tender passion made me, have pressed her to an immediate marriage, did not the dangerous illness of her grandmother forbid my being absolutely unreasonable & outrageous.

I fear, my dear father will not consider the match a prudent one; as the lady has neither money, nor expectations: but, as far as education, sound sense, virtue & beauty are concerned, I feel an honest pride in assuring him that she, whom I have selected for my wife, is every way worthy of being called his daughter. We are now in the fourth day of our public annual examination, & what with the excitement this causes me, what my courtship, & what correspondence I now am engaged in with Mr. Mackinnon, relative to the terms of my fresh engagement, I am scarcely in a condition to write you so long a letter as I ought on so important a subject but one thing I cannot omit. I found it necessary to lay one of my dear father's letters before the young lady & her only surviving parent to satisfy them that I was bound by no tie at home, & my happiness was very nearly nipped in the bud by the obstinacy with wh she refused to allow me to be the best judge as to the "prudence" or imprudence of our Union.

Miss Elizabeth Lewin is the eldest daughter (age 20) of a retired officer in the service of the late Begum Samroo, but now residing here with his family & to his character for uprightness & integrity his brother officers bear the highest testimony. Her only brother, a fine young fellow of 18, is an assistant in the school, under me. She will, I trust, be my wife long ere I can receive any reply to this, & as I am not a man to bestow merely a partial confidence on her, when, after an intimate acquaintance of many months, I have selected as the partner of my joys & cares, must request that any friends at home will refrain from signifying their disapproval, if they cannot approve my choice, & also from all allusion to the warmer blood, wh runs in her veins. Her cheek is but little less fair than my own dear Bell's but I fear to see it tingling with shame at any thing, wh may appear to point at an accident of birth, & have perhaps that wh your own sentiments & feelings would have suggested to yourselves.

Our examination has gone off admirably & among the visiters[sic] noticed Miss Georgina Jeremie. Adieu. I am too excited to add more than my love to Sarah & kisses to all yr dear children. Both love & duty to my dear father, to whom I cannot write till next month; & wishing Bell & Margaret all health, happiness & good husbands with all brotherly affection & sincerely I remain, my dear Nicholas,

Your sincerely attached brother,
M. Fitzf Monk.

P.S. We have just got China news, but no letter from Henry. The war there is ended. 21 millions of dollars to be paid as an indemnity to us, three towns, including Chusan, to be given in pledge, & trade open according to the law of nations. Major Uniacke R.M. was killed in the attack on "the City of Canals" & five other officers. The Cornwallis (Hal's ship) piloted by a steamer, led the attack squadron up the river.

The attesting witnesses of the Power of Attorney are both residents of Mussoorie. We have no notary nor consul. The principal civilian James Brewster Esq is Acting Political Agent & Judge "A.P.A." of the District, & the attached seal is the sea of his court. Wax is never used in India—the climate will not allow it. I shd have sent an affidavit, attesting the document but recollected & was told that voluntary oaths are now illegal in England. In this country one can swear till he is black in the face & then not be believed. God bless you all.

LETTER XXV

From MAUGER MONK, Mussoorie,
To HUGH MONK, Ann's Place, Guernsey.

14 NOVEMBER 1842

My Dearest Father,

I know not how to express sufficiently my gratitude for the readiness you have always shown to forward my views & the confidence you have placed in me by so readily acquiescing in my request as you have done. Ere your bounty arrived I had made an offer of my hand to one, on whom I had long previously bestowed my best affections, & if Miss Elizth Lewin be poor, she is the only girl I have seen in India, to whom I could have trusted my happiness, or that is likely to make my mountain home, what I require it to be, a comfort to me. My work is very heavy, but while I enjoy health & strength, I never grumble; & as they (it) prevented me seeking that society, without which life becomes a mere existence of drudgery, I have selected as my wife, one whom I am sure will prove a cheerful partner of my joys & woes, a daughter I do not feel ashamed to present to my father. Your blessing on our union, which takes place on the 26 inst, I make bold to anticipate. My own savings have been ample to provide every necessary comfort for my wife, without at all encroaching on your bounty, which I have made arrangements for laying out at 8 per cent. Immediately Messrs Cockerill & Co. have handed over the amount, until I find favourable opportunities of purchasing according to my original intention. Had Messrs Drummond drawn the letter of credit on themselves, as I wished, I could have disposed of it here to the Mussoorie Bank at a high premium; for the shuffling agents at Calcutta returned my bills, which were properly drawn, to have them on their own printed forms ostensibly, but in reality to gain a month in the hope of the rate of exchange, which has been high, becoming during that period in their favour. I followed your directions in enclosing the "power of attorney" to Nicholas, & would have you repeat to him those thanks, which I last month conveyed to him myself. And now, my dearest father, remember I am sincerely in love with one, who is most exigeante, & whose attractions of a superior order must plead with you as an apology for the brevity of this, which I enclose in one more full to my dear Bell. God preserve you in health, & may you yet find every member of your family a comfort to your declining years is the heartfelt prayer of

Your dutiful & most affectionate son,
M. Fitzh Monk.

LETTER XXVI

From MAUGER MONK, Mussoorie

To ISABELLA MONK.

[Endorsements:] "Per Overland Mail via Falmouth." "Landour November 16.Paid 12 as" "Guernsey Ja 16 1843"

14 NOVEMBER 1842

My Dearest Bell,

I seldom lose an opportunity of writing home but with considerable regret, so, if every mail brings not a letter from me, set it down to the score of my onerous duties, & they are really heavy. Adventurers, particularly from North Britain, seldom grant sinecures, & the gentleman I serve is certainly not one of those who would give a high salary to an idler, which, thank Heaven, whatever I once was, I am not now disposed to be, more especially as the 26th will see me a happier man in the possession of one, whose virtue, beauty & accomplishments are such as no merits of mine entitle me to—in short, my dear sister, I am to be married that day & am about to enter the "holy state" with a fairer prospect of happiness than seems generally to attend the ill-assorted marriages of Ind. I have raved enough to you about the young lady in many of my previous letters, & believe that in my last I was endeavouring to convince you of my philosophical indifference to one, who for the last ten months has filled my thoughts both sleeping and waking & I verily believe that within eight & forty hours after the despatch of that very letter was pouring into a not unwilling ear the story of love. Miss Elizabeth Lewin, my Bessy, is the eldest of the two daughters of one, who is reputed to have been the only honest man in the service of that old hag, the late Begum Sumroo of Sirdhana, one of whose battalions he commanded. Tho' never an extravagant man, he has saved nothing, for he was never known to take a bribe; but the education he has bestowed on his daughter & her own naturally excellent temper will contribute far more to the happiness of a person in my situation, than the possession of a fortune, without those essentials, which I must have to make my home a comfort to me. My dear father has furnished me with the means of making & saving money, tho' previous to the arrival of this bounty I had put by sufficient to make everything comfortable for the reception of my bride, who has just completed her twentieth year & refused sixteen, most of them really excellent offers, when I fairly wooed & won her. I know no one at home to whom I can liken her. What I recollect the youngest of Sir Wm. Call's daughters at the Plymo balls to have been, comes nearer than the features of any one I can call to mind at the moment. When you write to us, pray make no allusions to my fickleness, as you have been pleased to term it, for the little body, tho' as fair as yourself, possesses a vein of warmer blood, which is apt to kindle if she is led to think that any one of my affections may be wandering elsewhere and some of your random shafts might induce suspicion without the slightest ground for it.

The China War is now at an end, but I know not whether all the fleet returns. The Blonde, Modeste & Herald take home 6 millions of dollars. I heard from Hal just after the expedition against Nanking. His letter is dated the 21st July, but only reached me on the 21st Oct: three months after it was written. He improves visibly in each of his letters & I am truly happy to find is doing well, being now on board the Algerine, 10 Gun-brig, (a class of ships, which I believe carry no surgeon) & as he somewhat triumphantly writes, "sole medico". Strange to say, the day after his letter arrived, one from William took me quite by surprise dated "Off Penang, Malacca, Sep. 7th". He appears, & his tale bears the impress of truth, to have undergone many hardships in N.S. Wales, more particularly in a professional visit to one of Mrs. Harper's cattle stations on the Namoi, & tho' he had lots of patients, to have made nothing by them. The Himalaya was on her way to China, whence she returns to Europe via St. Helena. I have written to him most seriously, & another letter will meet him at St. Helena, & pointed out the inutility of his returning home, & perhaps, what I should not have mentioned without very good grounds, that he is not unlikely to find himself in a debtor's prison shortly after landing. He mentions his decided intention of returning to N.S. Wales to settle & intimates a wish that I would join him there but my nest is made, & all I have now to do is to feather it to the best of my ability. My home is in the Himalaya. It would perhaps have been as well had you, knowing Wm.'s jealous disposition, forwarded my letters to him unopened. He taxes others with being suspicious, while a jaundiced spirit breathes thro' his whole epistle. Adieu, my dearest sister, my own prospect of happiness has for the time made me quite selfish & heedless of the welfare of others. My curiosities are all in readiness for being packed off, but my own affairs oblige me to defer sending till the holydays. Serve out cake & wine to the health, happiness & prosperity of your dear brother & his beautiful bride. With all sorts of love & kisses to Sarah, Margaret, Aunt Eliza & Aunt Wm. (to whom next mail), Uncles Joseph & Wm. & Sal's worthy mate & their dear children, and sincerest prayers for the health of you all, particularly my dearest father, to whom my best duty & most sincere love, I am ever, my darling sister,

Your truly loving brother,
M. Fitzh. Monk.

LETTER XXVII

From MAUGER MONK, Mussoorie
To SARAH MAGRATH.

15 DECEMBER 1842

My Dearest Sarah,

We broke up last night for our annual vacation and the first day of the holidays I devote to you; for, seeing that I am now Benedict, and as happy and comfortable as my dear little wife and every collateral external circumstance can make me, I feel that you, above all, are likely to rejoice with me, knowing, as you do, all the sweets and delights of matrimony and all the nameless little etcetera, which enter into the jouissances of a married life. Every newly-spliced individual swears his wife is an angel, and tho' I cannot discover my Bessy's wings, I am not disposed to go out of the beaten track, did not calm reflection convince me that I have wooed and won one, deserving not only a handsomer, but a better man than your ever-loving brother. She is, however, so well pleased with him as to express the greatest disinclination to change him for another, and altho' better may possibly exist, she has neither seen them nor knows she where to look for them.

My most grateful thanks, my dear sister, for your well-intentioned endeavours to serve me, which I fear the distance between us prevents and will ever prevent, my being able to avail myself of. I doubt not that your friend Mrs. Major Rybot is both clever and sensible, but there is always more beneath the surface of the high-caste covenanted servant's lady than the straightforward mind of one, who has never been in India, can fathom, in short, more than you would dream of seeking—a feeling of local-prejudice—pride, which, repressed or smothered whilst in England, bursts forth with renewed vigour when re-transported to Indian ground. There is one question you might put to her, but I know she dare not answer it with candour. "Would you receive as an equal my brother, who is a schoolmaster in the Himalayas?" Her assent she may or might possibly give, and on returning to the country pretend to fulfil her promise by doing that, to which no member of the community to which I belong will submit, by patronising me. We are too useful to the covenanted to yield them homage as a superior class, we make them pay heavily for the services we consent to yield, and are shielded from insult by an independence of mind and action, which has always in the outset checked every attempt at insult or aggression. In short, we are wanted, and the proudest among them will stoop to ask for what he cannot otherwise obtain.

As to your other question to the good lady, relative to the probable success of a school in the Himalaya, it is no longer problematical. Thank providence, the seminary at Mussoorie is a flourishing establishment and your affectionate Mauger one of its thriving members, happy in the arms of a loving wife, in the training of a tolerably manageable set of young urchins, in the enjoyment of good health, a good climate and as many comforts as a moderate income can afford.

You see now what a contented old fogey I am becoming, without the remotest ambition of wearing a surplice or donning any thing over my scholastic toggery, save that which becomes a good and genuine sports-man. In testimony of which I am off early to-morrow to take a house in some well stocked neighbourhood, not many miles from this, and relieve the monotony of my daily duties by an unrelenting war on the denizens of the jungle during the vacation. By the bye, tell your right good fellow of a husband that his intimations respecting birds reached me too late for the present season. From the middle of June to January they are either bare-breasted or in blood-feather and unfit for stuffing during that period, except with sage and onions etc. He shall have a lot next holidays, and those which I have shall be despatched the instant the packing case, for which I have sent, arrives. My courtship and a somewhat heavy season of work prevented me giving them as early attention as I could have wished.

Yes, Sarah dear, by all means let me have the *London Illustrated* news, monthly by the Overland Mail otherwise, I shall not care much about them. Use your own discretion as to their being, in matter and engraving, worth the postage; for I have never seen the publication. I would that either your stock or Papa's could monthly furnish me with a good magazine or journal, which may combine scientific with a moderate portion of light reading, either historical or fictitious, or better still, connected with voyages and travels. And if any or either of you choose tri-monthly to pitch a quarterly at my head by the same conveyance (the Overland) I shall not grudge the postage of it in addition to the other. You know not what a craving I have to note the progress of literature, and what an appetite for scientific and general knowledge the imparting what little I possessed to others has given me.

Tell my dearest father, for whose health and happiness our daily prayers are offered, that, after considerable delay and shuffling on the part of the scoundrels at Calcutta, I have at length obtained £480 for my letter of credit for £500. Had it been drawn on Drummond themselves, I could have sold for £520 or £525, so you see, in pecuniary arrangements follow my directions, and don't let the bankers make a catspaw of you, in order to be able to place something to the credit of the Calcutta Agencies, the tenure of whose existence is indeed very frail. Had Cockerill's house smashed after the date of the letter of credit, I should not have realised a tithe of the amount, few of them ever paying a rupee in the £. Calcutta credit in the Upper Provinces is very low indeed. Now, don't call this a growl, my love but lead all at home to believe that I am no bad hand at the finance department, and don't like to see the Ditcher brokers putting £40 or £45 comfortably in their pockets, when it might have gone into mine. I have made my darling Bess so well acquainted with you all at home that she almost thought she could have dictated a sentence, but on coming to the point her courage has failed her and tho' she feels more, bids me for the present offer her love and sincere prayers for all your welfares, adding thereto her duty and affection to dear Papa. Happy myself, and still happier to hear that you & your dear children are thriving & comfortable in your new abode. I am too full at present to do more than invoke every blessing on the head of you & yours & our dear sisters & father. I shall write Aunt Wm. in Jan.

Your ever affectionate brother
Mauger.

P.S. No news of Wm. or Hal since last I wrote.

MERCHANT AND HOTELIER
1843

LETTER XXVIII

From MAUGER MONK, Mussoorie

To MARGARET MONK, Ann's Place, Guernsey.

14 FEBRUARY 1843

Valentine's day, my dear Margery, & a proper time to make amends for not having addressed a letter to your own sweet self for many a long month, tho' you know most of my letters home bear the Cornish motto for "one and all". I ought to have written last month; but my dear little wife & I were on a holiday-trip from wh we have returned in good time for the opening of the school campaign on the lst Feb, & though I was continually talking of you all & introducing Bess, by description, to every individual of the family, the days passed so quickly & pleasantly that I let the latest day for the last "overland" slip by unheeded. A description of the trip of a newly-married couple wod be rather mawkish to all save the parties interested, so I'll spare you the infliction of our little communings, & all the various nothings-to-any-one-else, those indescribable somethings, wh add a piquante flavour to our cup of real happiness. You can't conceive what a beneficial effect matrimony has had on me. I no longer mope in my solitary apartments, building evanescent castles, nor, in a fit of the blues, rest my chin upon my hand, looking the picture of discontent, & wish myself & all about me any where but where I am. My meals are cheerful, my leisure hours are enlivened, a smile & a kiss await my return from my tutorial duties, & as I sit by my snug fireside of an evening my darling Bess reads to me as I draw, or sits opposite to me with her work, if other avocations or studies require my attention. In short, I have now one, who can sympathise with my griefs or vexations, & rejoice when I rejoice; who has filled a vacuum I had long felt and which was fast hastening to make me a morose, dissatisfied fellow. We came upon no wonders during our jaunt, nor met with any adventures worth recording. My gun of a morning did its wonted good service, not only stocking our larder with game, but enabling me to make such presents as were acceptable to those, whom I find it my interest to conciliate. We visited one remarkable spot, the dripping cliff at Sansudtara, in one of the huge ravines wh branch off from the base of our range, & brought away several specimens of the petrefactions, wh abound there, the water possessing properties similar to those of the dripping well at Knaresboro' in Yorkshire.

This winter has been a tolerably mild one, and altho' I find that your's set in somewhat early & precious stormy, trust that you all & particularly my dear father have experienced no ill effects from its severity, if severe it has ultimately proved. Tell dear Papa with many thanks & my sincerest love, that awaiting a favourable opportunity of purchasing an estate, I have lent the money he so kindly & readily advanced me on undeniable security (real) at 10 per cent, the current rate of interest in the N.W. Provinces altho' I believe at Calcutta 12 per cent is the ordinary rate of charge.

You may be sure the coming mails are expected anxiously by me, & that by the latter end of March I hope to have received a good stock of congratulations on my change of condition; & it is not improbable that I may by that time have it in my power to announce the probable addition of one to the no of your nephews & nieces in due course of time. I have written to Clapton also by this mail ...

P. S. I have had no news either from Wm or Henry since I last wrote. I am about sending a letter to meet the former at St. Helena.

LETTER XXIX

From MAUGER MONK, Mussoorie

To HUGH MONK Esq. R.N., Ann's Place, Guernsey. Channel Is. Per Overland Mail, via Fal mouth. [Stamped:] "Landour Jun 13 6 as" "Guernsey Au 10. 1843" [Endorsed by H.M.] "Rajpore Dehra Dhoon"

15 MAY 1843

My Dearest Father,

Here I am having just entered my 29th year settled for life, a contented fellow with an excellent wife and, thanks to your bounty, an admirable estate with good prospects of increase in both, and I feel proud to add, thankful to the almighty for his many mercies & the protection he has extended to me in a land, the graveyard of many of Britain's sons, but where I have been truly blessed with uninterrupted health. At the foot of the Mussoorie range, about 3500 feet or rather more above the level of the sea, stands the village of Rajpore, elevated above & commanding an extensive view of the heavenly valley of the Deyrah Dhoon; and in the highest part of that stands the newly purchased estate of your affectionate son, who, sincerely happy at recognising your well-known hand in the last letter he opened from home, and at finding you much improved in health, dares not give vent to his feelings, lest, the cynical vein being uppermost, you should attribute his enthusiasm, not to the letter, but its enclosure. My engagement here is fast drawing to a close, never to be renewed. I have better prospects on my own estate, where as on most border stations my life will be principally mercantile with a dash of the agricultural & timber dealer. "Ich dien" to quote our favourite, Horace, "Tradam protervis in mare Creticum Portare ventis" but should it be my fate ever again to be a servant, it shall not be in the employ of any "Scot, that ever yet was born," the proud, unfeeling, selfish vagabonds, whose God is 'siller', whose sweetest savour 'stinking pride'. Should I ever, by my exertions, be able to realise the value of a saw-mill (I have water power in abundance) my fortune is made. Government gives timber for the clearing of the land, & takes no rent till it is cleared, but with clearing I have as yet nothing to do, nor do I intend to for some time.

Borax & wax I hope to make monopolies and am making arrangements with the wealthy Calcutta house, whose Commission Agent I am to be, to supply that market with turpentine and cedar oil, the former for the shipping, the latter for the government studs & mounted branches of the army. I know not whether it is used at home in farriery, here, it is found to be a most valuable medicine. Wax will in another year give me an income equal to that I derive from the school.

I have just despatched a case to Calcutta, containing birds, butterflies, beetles & other objects of natural histy together with three tippets, one each made of the feathers of the Golden Pheasant, and one for my dear little niece Nell, of the beautiful feathers of the Argus. I'll send Bell or Aunt an invoice list next mail, & sincerely do I regret that I can see nothing in this part of the world, which I could send as a present, that is not procurable cheaper & better at home. The handsomest Cashmere [?] shawls sold in the country were proved almost to mathematical demonstration to be of Glasgow manufacture. What I have sent have been mostly procured by the sweat of my brow, & the accuracy of my aim, & as they possess no great intrinsic value in themselves, will, I hope, will [sic] be considered as not procurable for "money". Bell's hint to me to get my darling to write first I cannot act upon, for reasons to you, who are well acquainted with the feelings on points of etiquette (eat-a-cat, my father-in-law jokingly calls it) of the West Indian ladies, sufficiently obvious.

My head is now full of business, and my heels too, for I have need to be active. The farming & other stock, carts, horses &c &c have all to be inspected, as the late worthy proprietor is off to Belfast with a moderate fortune of his own making & a handsome one to which he has succeeded waiting his arrival at home. All estates here are registered with all claims on them, so we can escape the tediousness of the law in settling purchases & from the admirable arrangements of the late commission, the boundaries of each are marked by pillars. To remove his neighbour's landmark is about the highest moral crime an Eastern can commit.

Adieu, my dearest father, my darling & I offer our daily prayers for your health & happiness and for that of our dearest brothers & sisters, either at home or abroad. Our sincerest love & kisses to them all & forget not, prithee, to present my dutiful love to my Uncles & Aunts & believe me to be, with the sincerest affection,

Your dutiful and loving son,
M. Fitz. Monk.

LETTER XXX

Mortgage.

15 JUNE 1843

Mauger Fitzhugh Monk of Rajpore, Dehra Dhoon, Bengal is bound to William Moorhead of the same place in the sum of 28,000 Company's Rupees at 8 per cent. £1,400 to be repaid within six years. Collateral: the Victoria Hotel Estate, consisting of 4 bungalows with stabling and out offices & former Dak bungalow, all about 4 acres, recently purchased by Monk from Moorhead.

LETTER XXXI

From W. MOORHEAD, Landour [?]
To M. F. MONK, Victoria Hotel, Rajpore.

20 JUNE 1843

My Dear Monk,

I am glad to hear you are well employed. I was all over Landour yesterday in search of a house. I could had [sic] "Kheen Ghur" at my own rent but that it is out of the doctor's beat. Those chaps have no conscience when making out a bill of charges!!

On my travels I met with very many of my old customers and was highly pleased to hear one and all express great satisfaction with not only what they experienced themselves but their "friends" spoke so favourably of you.

Well I succeeded in getting a house in the spot I wanted, near the hospital and as Mrs. Moorhead will come without a cook in her pocket, I shall feel very much obliged if your "Knight of the Spoon" will get me a man who can cook "dak bhat" & fry a beef steak. Anyone at all for a time!

Madame T has been puckerlousing again—why I'll swear Col. Roberts never went there of his free will. He was with me last year and his relative here Captn Roberts w'd not put his foot in the "filthy place", to my knowledge. But there is one satisfying thought that Col. R and many others whose arrival she may report but to her great mortification not their departure. I dare say they will be after boring Mrs. Moorhead. Don't tell the servants any thing about Mrs. Moorhead's coming so that Madam T might be on her guard against stopping the palkees. Do you take. If the bearers lay their [?] I'll make a great noise about it, but if your servants know any thing of the matter they will tell Jones and Thessones [?]. W. M.

Compls to Mrs. Monk.

Your's [sic] sincerely,
W. Moorhead.

LETTER XXXII

From W. MOORHEAD, Mussoorie
To M. F. MONK, Victoria Hotel, Rajpore.

27 JUNE 1843

My Dear Monk,

I was at Landour on Sun when your note arrived here. James continues pretty well and I am quite "myself again". I am glad to hear you are going it so fast. You will soon put down all opposition I hope. I have the pleasure to send the books. Yesterday Mrs. Moorhead wrote to me saying it is reported here that Mr. Monk wants to sell the Victoria; if so, let me know by return of post for the information of [sic]. I suspect the report is unfounded? I must again trouble you for the loan of Davy Dheen to take this letter to B[?]. The dft is gone back but Harvey has plenty of Dibs & not sparing of them. Compls to Mrs. Monk.

Yours sincerely,
W. Moorhead.

P.S. I'll be down in a week, or so ... I should take it as a great favour if you would send up to Rennick a score or two of fowls ... They are buying fowls for James daily and this is not right ... as I do this to offer R payment for Jame's [sic] keep would be thought an insult! Big or little, many or few kindly send what you can as soon as you like & charge them to W. M.

LETTER XXXIII

From W. MOORHEAD, Mussoorie [?]
To M. F. MONK, Rajpore.

29 JUNE 1843

My Dear Monk,

The enclosed concerns you. Introduce yourself politely! I will be down on Monday evg kindly have a Baste [sic] at Nullah pannee for me at 5 o'clock. I have my own saddle and bridle Mrs Moorhead is coming up! She will be at Rajpore early on Tuesday Morng. Farther particulars when I go down. By the by you must lend us a few old chairs, a table and a cot or two. My own cot will do for one and if you will tell the Jemadar to put some common "russee" in the large cot which I left you unfinished in the verandah of the billiard room, it will do admirably for all the children, except the infant. I am taking a small house on Landour to be near the hospital on James's account.

Yours sincerely,
W. Moorhead

P.S. Davie Deen might be taking a walk to Deyrah for the good of his health and you would give him these bills. Keep Mr. Thomas & the memo till I see you. I have a Dft on Deyrah for 233-4 which with some on the Mussorie Bank I will take down to you. W. M. Anything of that Lieut ... Hse. I forget his name who wanted a house?

LETTER XXXIV

From W. MOORHEAD, Landour [?]
To M. F. MONK, Rajpore.

N.D. JULY 1843 [?]

My Dear Monk,

I have the pleasure to send you the strong shoes, and the best servant in this world! I know you will appreciate his value. A rupee or two a month is nothing besides gents speaking of good servants is of itself sufficient to raise the name of any establishment. "Servants very attentive" you will observe "never here"; whereas I have been often told that Foden's[?] servants, even look'd impertinently!!

I hope you have sent the pigeons[?] fowls, drawers (the new ones!) &c for me, and when Mrs. Moorhead's trunk arrives tomorrow(?) by two coolies, kindly tell them not to halt at Raipore. They shall be paid extra. The children's flannels are in the trunk!

I quite forgot my ink. All of course taken from you in this way shall be returned, save and except such things as ink, which I am sorry I can't promise to return! otherwise than expended.

Will you kindly look at Captn. Fisher's account for about 6/8 or 7/8, and give me ever so roughly a memo of it. I sent him a copy which he has lost and wants another. He has a page in the ledger, I think.

When making out your statement just put down the amount of 10/- Messrs Thomas, Sissmore, &c, &c. You are much surer of their cash than if you had it in your bag! And it will save you the trouble of another memo and some "entries"!!

Your's sincerely,
W. Moorhead.

P.S. Mrs. Moorhead unites with me in kind regards to Mrs. Monk & yourself. And I have the pleasure to send Bowyers Map also a remembrancer for Mr. French.

LETTER XXXV

From W. MOORHEAD, Landour [?]
To M. F. MONK, Rajpore.

24 JULY 1843

My Dear Monk,

I have only one kimdee [?] from you. You kindly emptied another for me but I put the stuff in a clothes basket.

If you get the amt of this dft or order in three days grace— well, but if not kindly send it back to me that I may "protest" it. Captn Baldock has been advised of the demand on him, and said he would be ready to meet it! (Also a dft on the treasury for 16/-) I will go down some day this week. I wish you could get Major Sweetenham's lowest word for the carriage tomorrow or next day. Say you think you can squeeze 200 Dibs, if he will "stand a treat".

I must put a few in the court of requests next month. They are all anxious for me to make their bills over to you, and one has gone so far as to say he will allow the percentage to be added to his ac. All this is very fair no doubt and I said I would consult you ---- [sic]. Captn Baldock I shall not hand over to any one, he shall pay myself or ---- [sic] I'll forgive him!

Now do like a good fellow send [... damaged ...] the palkee as soon as possible; [...] Davie Dhee be going, to Mussoorie send him on to Major Sweetenham.

Many thanks for your kind [...] of the Dak Bungalow, but as [...] be going down for a move to the 20th about the lst of September it is not worth while shifting over quarters till then, and I am so much nearer the "nobs"[?] here I can torment them more cheaply. I am annoying the very life out of some, not those that are "hard up" but those who are very "backward to come forward".

I have been advised to smoke the hookah. I think you have a rewanie [?] (or some such named) bottom which if you don't want and will put "my snake" to it, I will pay you for both. But mind if you have taken my snake into use or intend to use it I won't have it. It is only in the event of it being to you as it was to me, useless, that I will have the article! I sent to the bazar but failed in getting a decent turn out, so had to put up with an article which you hold in the hand. Our kind regards to Mrs. Monk & self.

Yours sincly,
W. Moorhead.

24th July. I have paid the bearer 2 aas for taking the trouble.

LETTER XXXVI

From W. MOORHEAD, Landour
To M. F. MONK, Rajpore.

2 AUGUST 1843

My Dear Monk,

I have the pleasure to send you Mr. Harvey's letter. The whip I would also send but it's a nice little one and I like the trouble of carrying it when on mare back. I'll charge you nil for its keep and deliver it free of expense one of these days—when I have no further use for it. There now! I'm sure you'll say thankee!!

Arrah then is it the pit to put the ice in you want to be after getting the plan of. Then that same thing I have got ready for you but can't send it today, but shall forward it to you by the lst proximo. It is safe in my own head! And I could not get it out in any sort of shape in reasonable time but you shall have it "clear as mud" when I go down.

I hope you are coming along with Mrs. Monk to the Ball & Supper at Mrs. Emile's "Rooms" tonight. Long [?] Ned Rendale is at the moment being spliced to someone at the depot—a girl I dare say, for I hear of only one widow here and she wants something handsome for her money. I now recollect the "Bride Elect" is the sister-in-law of the Qr. Mr. Sergt. (Ten Broske [?]) but I hope you'll be there, and see her. I am told she is a nice creature, and I am dying of anxiety to satisfy myself that what I have heard is not true. Rendale is a good-looking fellow, and goes about neat and clean, keeps a clean neat room and I am told his last love excels him, if possible, in all these points!!!

Goodbye, I must practice a few steps and look over "panes lasts[?]" etc. Our kind regards to Mrs. Monk & self.

Your's sincly,
W. Moorhead. Landour, 2nd August 1843.

By the bye, don't send Fords (Meerut return) palkee I must pay him for it! Keep it instead of one of those "absent accounted for". I'm writing to Ford I shall tell him you are about to pay me Rs.400 on his account, or perhaps I should say the Rs. 500, it being the even half thousand sounds better!

Kindly get 9/2 from the Chowdah for me or tell the Jemadar to do so. He knows for what. Doolie and Jampan hire Rs 5

A Cow 4-1

A balance 0-1

Total costs 9-2-0

And oblige W.M.P.S. I wrote to Jephson, four pages full, yesterday all about the Agency and Palmer's wines. I told Jephson you would take the latter for the supply of the intemperance society here provided he would ensure you a constant supply for the house. I have been speaking to Macguire who will do the needful! They consume 24 Doz. monthly. More anon.

LETTER XXXVII

From W. MOORHEAD, Landour
To M. F. MONK.

N.D. After 2 AUGUST 1843

My Dear Monk,

With much pleasure I send you the whip—I thought you had half a dozen of them. I only used it once (carried it!) my mare requires neither whip nor spur. I must run her against the swiftest in your stud for a bottle of champagne when I go down. There is nothing on the hills can beat her for half a mile on a level.

I could not get a pick of "Scotts" sticks—not John Scotts mind ye, I suppose his are still dearer—for less than one rupee, take many or few, so I applied to Rennick who got the dozen ready for a gent at the price he mentions. Of course we can say nothing of the great "upright & down straight" conduct evinced in the sale of what was promised to another gent!! Perhaps selected by himself!!!

We are much obliged for the mangoes, and have paid the coolie. I have no dread of being mulcted the 2,000 Dibs, perhaps I might be tired of "life at home" in three years hence and if so will be happy to give you much profit, a fair profit, on your bargain. Should the climate of Europe not agree with my half worn out constitution back I come, and join my capital to the fag end of some ones and set myself down for the rest of my life in the vicinity of these mountains. But certainly not so high up as Inra am, nor so low down as Dâk puth [?] but "between the two" as davy danced! On that spur of the Jenapannee Hill round which the new road was to, but never will run. (Govt may improve the road and perhaps take the line now proposed and the angle proposed, but will never widen it to the desired extent. Captn Graham the ex-officer said such a road might not cost less than 3 lac of Rs.) I have cast my eye. The owner wants to sell it badly, I hear.

I must have a talk with you about something of the kind when I go down on the lst I will spend a couple of days with you & make the ice pit. An hospl will be at Sansadanah you won' object, I should rather think! my last letter will bring out Jephson's mind as regards this branch of his business. Mrs. Emile is going to do great business next season. I don't know whether she can carry so extensively as she speaks of in the theatre, and of course I did not like to enquire! You should have come to the ball ... [sic]. I am too critical and therfore won't say a word, except that the supper wines, beer &c were superior, but thro' some mismanagement a knife or spoon was not to be had, by a bashful man like me, for any money, but that was not the fault of the host or hostess. The viands excelled anything I saw since I left Victoria. They were really good and was not that the more vexing when "manners" forbid the use of fingers!

Yours sincerely,
W. Moorhead.

P.S. Kindly send us that old grumbling tailor—Mrs. M is making coarse [?] togs for the little ones and is badly in want of an assistant!

LETTER XXXVIII

From W. MOORHEAD, Landour
To M. F. MONK, Rajpore.

17 AUGUST 1843

My Dear Monk,

Many thanks for your kind invite "some fine morning" I wish we may see one by the first of Sept, and then you may depend on seeing me. Like a decent boy send the enclosed to Mr. Powel.*

For me, and per bearer returning kindly let me have a "muster" of your Castillon brandy which is "largely" spoken of by Ford. And also my oak stick. I fell down a hill and broke the only I had, a present, and I don't fancy throwing away a rupee on a cudgel for half a month. Here's a hint. It strikes me that the advertisement of your drinks should form a part of the main one—people may read the one and forget the other, which wld then form a part of the accommodation offered—a "sine qua non" to many travellers. I know why 3,500 Dibs have been offered for the patch next the Loder's Bungalow. Captn H had the planning of it all. He told me last Feby that Loder was "giving up" in October! I'll tell you all about it when I go down. Don't break your shins after it. You will get all for a song before two years are over. Mind what I say. It is all the better for you if H does buy the patch next your estate! I'll tell you how but not to-day.

I expect a tombstone—commonly called a Headstone—from Delhie in a few days; kindly send it up on arrival and keep the two bullock Hackney, which brings it, to take my traps to Meerut.

I hear Sedgley has arrived. How does he look? As fat as ever?

Don't allow the Jemadar to take away any Farrier's Tools except a case of bleeding &c instruments. Don't tell him that I have written to you on this subject, but show him some dirty old list and say you bought all from me, and that if he takes anything away you will make me pay for the deficiency! And by not saying anything about consulting me, or the like, he will think you have a list which indeed I never had. But this I know the paring knives were made a present to me, and the firing irons, or whatever they are called, and other things were made up by me. Now go wisely to work as I don't know all he had this I know he wanted nothing, and he made some remark the day he was here about the implements. He does not know but there is a full list in my papers, which you may stumble on. Take all and let him claim them from me. Our kind regards to Mrs. Monk and yourself,

Yours sincerely
W. Moorhead.

*Did you get the Oak Bungalow register from him yet? How much will you take for the grey mule bought from my modest friend anonymous?

LETTER XXXIX

From W. MOORHEAD, Landour
To M. F. MONK, Rajpore.

20 AUGUST 1843

My Dear Monk,

Many thanks for the stick and the bottle of brandy --- yrs & the Dfhtee. Skinner had the option to return the palkee or keep it at 15 Rs. The other 10 Rs is the hire of it. I hope Ford won't charge me more than 15 Dibs for the one I gave you instead. What is it like? I am sorry to hear the Gents bungalow is so leaky; everyone knows it was not so last year except "Harris' room", as I told you. Had it been other I would have told you most certainly. I admire your modesty in wanting me to assist in the roofing you propose. I cannot discover (and I have been twice in front of the mirror, since I got your note) anything "green in my eye". No! No! My outlays at the Victoria are at an end. They were pretty considerable too, one way or another! I see you did not require my hint about the advertisement. But what has Indal Sing been up to? I thought him very honest. Have you got a billiard table in order yet? If so all the rain and fog imaginable won't keep me from Rajpore!! I'll tell you what Macguire says about the mule in my next. An army will be formed I'm told. Our kind regards to Mrs. Monk and Self.

Yours sincerely,
W. Moorhead.

LETTER XL

From W. MOORHEAD, Meerut
To M. F. MONK, Rajpore.
[Stamped:] "Meerut 10 Sept. Paid 1 AS"

9 SEPTEMBER 1843

My Dear Monk,

To-day I had the pleasure to receive your note and a dft on Messrs Wm. Scott & Co. for cos two hundred, which makes five hundred on Ford's account. I was at his auction to-day and bought a capital nag (a very strong hill pony) for you, at 32 Dibs! Horses are going for a song here, and I doubt not but Ford will send you, with the pony perhaps, a couple of good cheap buggy horses.

I am much disappointed by finding my brandy, sherry &c still in Ford's stores unsold. He tried to get rid of some of it to-day, but it was "no go". There were no buyers. How I'm to act in this case I can't suppose. I must try the canteens with it.

At present I can say nothing about letting your 3,500 Rs stand but will write to you again in a few days. I will willingly let you have it at interest if I can do without it, but as to my having said you could renew the period of payment, your last note contains the first I heard of it. You may recollect on the contrary I said I should require the amount to settle with the firm below.

It was so wet yesterday I could not go see those gents whose promises I am depending on keeping me out of jail. If they disappoint me you may at once go into deep mourning, for,

Yours sincerely,
W. Moorhead.
Meerut, 9th September 1843.

P.S. Mrs. Moorhead joins me in kind regards to Mrs. Monk, Miss Lewin and yourself. We got safe here on the 7th—did not reach Seheranpore till 1 pm and Meerut at 3 pm! ! ! Saw nothing of the Gent [?] nor the stone. Send it to Rennick when you get it.

LETTER XLI

From MAUGER MONK, Rajpore

To HUGH MONK, Guernsey.

Per Overland Mail via Falmouth. [Stamped:] "Derah Doon 13 Sept 12 as".

"13 Nov 13 1843"

10 SEPTEMBER 1843

My Dearest Father,

But that I do not like to let the mail pass without a letter from me, & my darling wife is not well enough to-day to take that duty off my hands, I could have indulged an indolent mood with pleasure, & filled up the spare moments of the day with unsatisfactory reasons for not writing. Since, by your assistance, I have been able to start upon my own bottom & mark out a line of life of my own selection & in which I own no other master than the public, I have had no idle moment and as fast as I get one thing done, have another ready for me to direct my immediate attention to.

In addition to my regular business, which is that of a wine, timber & general merchant with a strong dash of the agriculturist, on that part of the estate which borders the high road, is an excellent hotel, carried on by my servants, but of which I am the acknowledged proprietor. This, without any trouble on my part, further than an occasional visit to stimulate the niggers & see that they don't help themselves is really a very profitable branch of my business & a spec on which I pride myself not a little, the more so, as it has proved the best card of introduction to my principal occupation. I have a large establishment of smiths, carpenters, saddlers & in fact I supply the wants of a large community to a large extent, & find my profits, allowing a fair remuneration for personal exertion to fluctuate between 15 & 25 per cent. But oh! That I who could not once bear to think of an operation, should at times find myself knee-deep in veterinary practice.

Manufacturing geldings is by no means uncommon, & a nice half-dozen of young frolicsome colts are sporting before me in the fields, waiting the departure of the monsoon to be reduced to the neuter gender. Of my instruments I can't say much, as you will judge when I tell you, I was once obliged, after throwing aside two scalpels, to finish opening a scrotum with my hunting knife. What I most require are bleeding & abscess lancets, bisterys, & scalpels, which if you can pick up cheap, would be very acceptable. A couple of each would do and might be sent overland. The operations for diseases in the chest I should not like to undertake, do shall not ask for trachars. My gunsmith has made up all the heavy tools I require. For emasculating a pony I get a gold mohur (£1.12), a horse or charger two. Without wishing to brag, I believe there are here few harder-working men than myself. Egad, I shall have need to be industrious. Bess promises to be prolific, & the next mail will, under Heaven, announce, I sincerely trust, her safe delivery of an heir to me, & a grandchild to you. May it prove a worthier child than its father, who has long bitterly repented the follies & errors of his youth, & would fain turn out, if not an excellent, at least an honest & worthy member of society.

Bell tells me you have been to London & had derived more satisfaction from your meeting with William than you anticipated, & that there is every chance of Hal's promotion …

Your affectionate & dutiful son,
M. Fitzh. Monk.

LETTER XLII

From MAUGER MONK, Rajpore, Dehra Dhoon
To ISABELLA MONK, Ann's Place, Guernsey.
Endorsed: Guernsey 14 Dec. 1843.

14 OCTOBER 1843

My Dearest Bell,

I've just discovered this to be the latest safe day for the Overland Mail & am in such a whirl I know not how to write. My dear darling was confined on the 26th Sept of a daughter, wh I deeply regret to say was seized with a series of convulsions, tho' going on very well for two days, & expired on the morning of the 29th. Poor Bess would have been my amanuensis to-day but for this untoward calamity, & as she is far from strong, I wod not let her write, to call her sorrows up afresh. I am almost ashamed to confess how much better I bear our loss than she does, but having no moment I can call my own, I have no time to brood. Obliged to discharge one assistant for drunkenness & another for peculation, I have to do all my own work at this the busiest season of the year, and this estate of mine, having as far as the outbuildings &c are concerned been constructed with the utmost disregard to convenience, by the time evening has set in, I am as completely knocked up as I can be. The comet has not been without its share of evil influence this wet season, for never did I see unceasing torrents pour for three months, as they have this, I hope, ended monsoon. So heavy was the rain that strong tiles were broken by it, & so unceasing that it required my unceasing attention to prevent the horses & cattle being affected by it. The roads, fields, everything was flooded, & now the sky is looking bright, I'm off to inspect & repair damage. "A stitch in time," you know the rest; so spare yourself the infliction. By the bye you lost a fine budget of letters when the Memnon with the July mails was lost off Cape Guardafui, & God knows I've now no time to repair that damage. We received the papers, but no letters last month. His & Bess's love to the family.

LETTER XLIII

From ELIZABETH MONK. Rajpore

To HUGH MONK.

"Per over land Mail via Falmouth." "Paid".

[Stamped]: "Derah Doon 17. Dec. 6as" "14 Feb 1844"

[Endorsed]: Answered Feby 26th 1844."

17 DECEMBER 1843

My Dear Father,

I do not know if it is owing to my education or if timidity is natural to asiatics but though I have made several attempts I never could gain courage enough to write a letter to you. I hate preambles so I hope, my dear father, you will consider this as sufficient excuse for my neglect. It is my only one. And now though late allow me to offer you my no less sincere thanks for your late gift which now appears to have been laid out profitably. At first we had some doubts. One branch of Mauger's business is very disagreeable to him and he is thinking of giving up the hotel entirely if he can find a person capable of conducting it and as soon as he is better known as a merchant. In this capacity the hotel will be of great advantage to him if still conducted by somebody else.

We were very happy to hear of your excellent health both from Sarah and Bell's letters of last mail. You must find it a great blessing particularly after your last severe illness for none but those who have been ill can fully appreciate this one of heaven's greatest gifts.

I have from my childhood had one ailment or another, and to my own delicate health I attribute my poor baby's death. Others may be born to me and live but that will not restore to me my first born. Don't think me romantic, my dear father, my sorrow is not stale yet, though perhaps I ought not to indulge in it now. Mauger is gone up to Landour this morning and I expect him back in the evening. We have a sporting Parson here who has made him promise to go out shooting with him when I am afraid he will not return so soon. The late heavy fall of snow at Landour has driven "his riverence" down to Rajpore where he intends to remain till after Christmas. However, he is disappointed in his expectations of Mauger's joining him in his shooting excursions thanks to a great press of business continually for believe me I do not like his risking his neck amongst khuds, bears and leopards. His absense [sic] today makes me more busy than I would be if he were at home and as this is the last day for the Mail to start I shall write a few lines to Margaret whose dislike to letter writing seems to be almost as great as mine. With our united love believe me my dear father, your affectionate daughter, Elizabeth Monk. My dear Margaret, I now write you a few lines to introduce myself & induce you to write to me. Bell writes you are all quite well and in your next I hope we shall hear something of Henry, he ought to have arrived home before this. William we are sorry to hear remains so inactive in London, to Mauger he has not written since he heard of his marriage. Mauger is not very well to-day or would write himself and wish you all a merry Christmas but now you must allow me to do so for myself and him. Kiss all Sarah's little ones for us and tell them uncle Mauger and aunt Bessy wish them a very, very merry Christmas. Give our love to Sarah and Isabella and accept the same from,

Your affectionate sister
E. Monk.

"BEGGARED BEYOND REDEMPTION"
1844-1845

LETTER XLIV

From MAUGER MONK, Rajpore
To HUGH MONK, Guernsey.
"Per Overland Mail, via Southampton."
[Stamped]: "Deyrah Dhoon 17 Jan /44. 6 ans."
"Y 13 MR 13 1844" "Guernsey May 17 1844".

15 JANUARY 1844

My Dearest Father,

My inclination as well as my duty inclines me to address my first letter of the season to you, trusting sincerely that in spite of any bodily ailments you may yet live many, many years for us to look up to you & with fewer afflictions than you have of late been subjected to. Our Christmas would have been much more cheerful had we received any letters from home by the last overland mail, & out of Sarah's usual batch of newspapers two only have come to hand. We have had two or three gentlemanly letters from Capt. Bean, in all of which he desires to be particularly remembered whenever I am writing home. My dear Bessy's box is, I believe, en route; but we have no certain information since it was made over to my Calcutta agents. You must really pardon me, & so must my dear sisters & Aunt Wm if my letters home are fewer than they have hitherto been. My new line of life is as laborious a one as man ever undertook, & the more I extend my business, the more arduous is my task; for I cannot get a competent assistant, & like yourself in that respect, would not trust the best accountant with my cashbook & ledgers. My last additions to my business are the occupations or professions of tanner & exporter of hill produce, rather as a botanist than a cultivator. I have repeatedly asked in my letters the price of musk at home, particularly at the Apothecaries Hall. I can supply it far purer than any musk they may get from China but would like to know if there are any particular methods used or rather recommended for its presentation in the pod. Two species of Aconita, the Aconitum ferox (the most powerful poison in India) & the Aconitum heterophyllum are amongst my present exports to Calcutta. Are they in demand at Apothecaries Hall? And will you also kindly inquire for me the average selling prices in London of turmeric & borax. I am the only European merchant who has any direct communication with Thibet, and can/shall be able to furnish the latter article in almost any quantity in a twelve month from this time. All my trade in that quarter goes on by barter; for every pound of salt or alum I get one of borax, which is brought over the mountains on sheep, each of which carries about 26 or 30 pounds. While on business I would add that my leopard & bear skins (black or brown) are unequalled by any I have yet seen. Messrs.Young & Co. of Lime St. in the city, wine merchants & exporters, have been strongly recommended to me by Brigadier Roberts C.B. & other gentlemen. I should not object to accept a commission agency in the wine trade from them; for situated as I am midway between the winter & summer residences of the largest sanitarium in India I have a splendid opportunity of carrying on a business profitable to myself, beneficial to my principals & without detriment to any other agency I now or may hereafter hold. I purchased all the Brigadier's imported stock on his quitting the Himalaya, & sold it well & rapidly. The wines were very superior.

My poor Bess's health & spirits have suffered much from the death of our babe. I would try change of air, but that she will go nowhere without me & to quit my business even for a day is almost an impossibility. Talk of Guernsey artificers & their laziness. Had you the 70 or 80 native workmen, who are fairly making a fellow bawl his lungs to pieces, they drive you crazy in a week. Turning a brick over for five minutes is nothing to the scheming of these rascals, but I must after them. So, accept the sincere love & duty of myself, & my dear Bess, whose daily prayers are offered for yourself & my dear brothers & sisters. To those so dear to us, to me in particular & to Magrath's increasing circle (what fine fellows the boys must be, even allowing Sarah to paint their portraits) our united love, & kisses. My love to all my Uncles & Aunts & believe me, my Dearest Father,

Your ever affectionate & dutiful son,
M. Fitz. Monk.

1843-44

Some pages of a ledger, recording the bills run up by some of the residents of the Victoria Hotel, Rajpore. Their names include: Capt. Mackenzie, 2nd Eur. Regt., Jno. Mackinnon Esq., Genl Dennis, Lt. Col. Syers, 19 Regt. N. I., Miss Mackinnon, I. Barnes Esq. C. S., Capt. Pratt H M's 16th Lancers, Capt. Sleeman, F. Anderson Esq. M. D., Lt. Pennington 11 Regt N. I., Lt. Stallard, H. A., Lt Bleaymire 2 Eur Rg, E. Thomas Esq. C. S. Saharunpore, F. T. Boyd Esq (Capt), Asst. Comy. Genl.

LETTER XLV

From M. F .MONK, "Wick", Rajpore
To W. MOORHEAD. [Copy]

10 AUGUST 1844

My Dear Moorhead,

Fain would I try and be facetious, but from bad health, destruction of property and continued separations from my wife, rendered necessary by almost uninterrupted sickness, for I am half my time or more alone from her being forced to live up hill, I find my spirits unequal to a jest. Never perhaps in the annals of Rajpore has the Vic been so prosperous, & to my exertions and labours I attribute the illness, which has all but made an old man of me, commencing with an apoplectic stroke or coup de soleil on the 18th April last, since which date I have not been what I was. I have done all I could to dispose of the business and stock but ineffectually, for the benefit of the estate. As for European assistants, they have been nearly my ruin; and not one of the proposing tenants had even wherewith to purchase the stock in trade, tho' security was offered for the rent by some.

My principal object in writing now is to ascertain how far there is any probability of your return, or rather when that event may be expected, for I will then put a steady man and his wife in charge; but on this as well as the next proposal I must have a decided answer by return of the mail, my health being now to me a paramount consideration. You must ere this have decided on your future plans and arrangements, and thus I put it to you:

lst. In the event of your returning, I will from and after the receipt of your letter by next mail put a man in charge of the hotel in your name, leaving the hotel and out buildings (what is left of the latter) in their present state provided at the same time I am repaid the ready cash paid you on the estate and stock (liquors and wines not included, for I have been paying off as I could this amount to Mr. Jephson & will settle the rest with him).

2ndly. Should you not be returning, I propose to give you £700 sterling in lieu of all demands under the mortgage bond, & I will raise/obtain that amount and forward it to you immediately on receiving your consent to receive it.

The principle of honour is so strong in me, that I have had a severe with myself on the subject but as I will now show you I do no injury to that principle, and consider my own and my wife's health of some weight and moment in this matter.

In the first instance, you agreed in the event of your return to take back the place reimbursing any expences I may have been at in maintaining of it, & consequently I consider my first proposal honest & fair, as I cannot carry the business on any longer.

In the 2nd so fearful have been the autumnal monsoons (43 & 44) that the palkee godowns have been supported on props and the walls crumbling away hourly. The roof of the Gentlemen's bungalow is tottering to its fall inwards, and so harrowing a sight is the continued leakage, that I am almost driven crazy by the everlasting complaints of having got the rheumatism from the rain streaming into some gent's ear while asleep, and messages to look at tents & "be good enough Mr. Monk to send up my horses, your stables leak dreadfully," &c &c. To replace the fallen buildings, new roofs (thatch) the bungalows, stables and out houses has been calculated by measurement to be at lowest about 4100 Rs and on this I have grounded my offer, not taking into consideration the loss I have suffered from customers leaving me in consequence of the heavy leakage.

In the event of neither proposal being acceded to, I shall after the season has ended sell off stock & furniture, close the hotel, and leaving a chowkedar in charge give you regular notice to enter on the bond, which you know under ordinary circumstances you could not do for the next five years. I have laid these proposals before men considered upright, and under the circumstances detailed herein they have been pronounced as fair as could be to both parties, & consequently I feel less hesitation in offering them, tho' sorry to be compelled to do so more by the effects of climate and weather than my own volition. Trusting all your family are well & with best respects to Mrs. Moorhead, believe me

Yrs sincerely
M. F. Monk.

LETTER XLVI

From MAUGER MONK, Landour
To Dr. HUGH MONK R.N., Ann's Place, Guernsey.
Per Overland Mail, via Southampton.
Endorsed: LL 8 Jan 1845.

17 NOVEMBER 1844

My Dear, Dear Father,

Heaven has blessed myself & my dear, darling Bess with a son, the first grandchild, I believe, unless Wm has been beforehand with me, who can legitimately bear the name of Monk. Thanks to the same almighty providence, we had no Scotch surgeon, who, as in the case of our former babe, preferred a ball room to a fee (for few/none will accouch under 100 Rs) & gave the Mother laudunum to retard her accouchment.

Dr. Mackinnon, tho' of the same origin as the last I engaged, a Bruce forsooth, was kind & attentive beyond belief. He, however, is a Dorsetshire man, accustomed to soldiers & warfare, but not the less kind to the fair sex on that account. Heretofore he never would receive fee or reward from me & I have some doubts whether he will now, but take it he must, or I shall get vexed with him. It is not the custom to offer it till the mother is pronounced convalescent & able to get out of bed so I have not yet tried him.

On the occasion I would ask as I am always asking something, a good strongly bound Bible in wh I may record my family with the dates certified by the clergyman. They are continually changed, but if you will give me a Bible, I can get both my marriage, & the birth, & I trust, the baptism certified. Poor Bess was confined at 4 am, in the morning of the 14th Novr & was scarcely one hour before all was over. Tho' very ill yesterday (milk fever) she is now doing well. The boy is a strong lusty fellow & is to be named, (you need not ask why, for the first name is my own selection) "Henry Lewin Monk". I therefore ask for the Bible, a large one, in conformity with the custom of India, Church records being perishable from white ants, & consequently unavailable. Be it ever so heavy send it overland "to be forwarded by Bhangy Dak on arrival & direct to Landour," the sanitarium of the Himalaya, only 10 miles from my late place of residence, & 5 from Mussoorie, tho at 7,250 feet above the level of the sea. Direct in future "Landour, Himalaya Mountains, Bengal". I have opened a school on my own account with every prospect of success & enjoying my health in the finest climate in the Himalaya besides the profits derivable from the sale of my drawings. Were I over-sanguine I shod say, I could retire well at the end of seven years but the matchlock wound through both ancles renders me a cripple for nearly three weeks yearly, & tho' I believe all the bits of copper have passed out, yet the slightest indulgence on my part will reproduce an opening of some kind. Dr. Mackinnon says the "newly invented stocking" will prevent a recurrence of it, if I live at regular hours & on low diet. I shall do so now, but could not before, when I breakfasted sometimes at 6—next day at 11—& dined the former time at 1, & the second, could not return to dinner till 7 or 8. I have had no occasion to call a meeting of my creditors. They are all aware that I have been unremitting in my exertions, tho' they willingly admit that some of my specs (suggested, by the bye, by themselves) were ill-judged. Since I last wrote to you & before to Bell about the loss of my crops &c by locusts, I have lost my credit as a horse-breeder from the introduction, I know not how, of glanders into my stables. How they came there, (for cleaner & more open ones exist not in India) I cannot conceive, but, perhaps, previous to the reduction of that branch of my establishment, I may have offended a certain class, by referring one gent to my native rough-rider (chabook suwar) & then knocking the young puppy off his poney for insolence. No matter, the existence of the disease I fully, to my horror, proved by inoculation, tho' I had disbelieved its existence in the East. As the discovery hurt my pride, so did I feel it more deeply than my loss but I was too honest to disavow what I knew to be true, & when questioned, openly avowed that such had been the case & that I had destroyed five of my own horses in consequence. However, my dearest father, these losses have led to one discovery, that the talents, with wh God has blessed me, & the education, wh you have at a heavy sacrifice, vouchsafed are more available capital without risk of loss, than the speculations into which my presumption led me. One thing, however, harasses me. I know not by what honourable means to escape the schemes & machinations of that low-bred Belfast Orangeman, Moorhead. He has taken me in, & tho' I have served him in the same way to a certain extent by drawing up the mortgage bond myself in such a manner as to prevent his interference with me for six years from the lst July 1843, yet I do not sit easy under it, knowing what he is, & that I shall have to play the scoundrel at a scoundrel's game. It's what I cannot now do tho' I must, supported only by the belief that treachery must be met by the same weapon, one I am not used to wield. I'd sooner meet him with cold steel. For myself I care not, but I hope before the first of December to have secured an asylum for my darling & her babe & one hour's ride will carry me out of the reach of the unrelenting Orangeman or his myrmidons; for my best, most tried & trusty hill-nag is not, whilst I can maintain him, to be bought for gold & less space of time than that will carry me out of the Company's territories. I'll give him leave to find me in Gurwhal if he dare follow. I once before asked whether you could ascertain the prices at Apothecaries Hall of borax Thibet (sohaga), musk, aconitum ferox (atees) & aconitum heterophyllum (bresh). The two latter I procure cheap & sell to the native princes at a tremendous profit, as poisons, but in small quantities. Musk brings me in at Calcutta on an average 30 Rs for about 2 drams less than an oz & sometimes more. From the time the deer is killed it is never out of the sight of myself or Wilson, & our musk is preferred before even that of China. It is tested here with either garlic juice (lusson) or assafoetida (hing.), in a solution of wh a string is first soaked, then dried, & passed thro' with a needle & the string. I must now close, for I have again unpleasant news from my place below, so with love to my dearest sisters, Magrath's bairns & William when writing, in fact, to all enquiring relatives & friends, Believe me,

Ever yr affectionate & dutiful son,
M. Fitzh Monk.

P.S. I hope to be in better spirits next mail.

8 January 1845.

Complaint from Major-General Sir James Dennis at Fort William, about being overcharged by "Mr. Monk an Innkeeper at Rajpore" for a "room not fit for the residence of any Gentleman from its extreme filth and being nearly uncovered to the roof and the ceiling cloth hanging down immediately over the bed place". He declares his refusal to pay the balance of Rs 83 allegedly owing.

LETTER XLVII

From W. MOORHEAD, Minore House, Drum, Clones.

To M. F. MONK, Mussoorie.

16 JANUARY 1845

My Dear Monk,

Your favour I duly received—3 months ago—up to this moment I know not what to make of the communication, unless I put it down as a jest. You complain of my selling the place too dear to you and the like!!!! And that you would be disposed to pay me down half, besides paying the balance due on your note of hand! A very modest offer, truly. I certainly would like to get any money due to me in Bengal, forwarded to this country, where I have use for it and have written to Messrs. Jephson & Co. on that subject, but I should not like to make the sacrifice you speak of nor will not.

You say your business is doing well, I'm glad of it. That your health is not good I am sorry to hear that. Rajpore was considered a very healthy place, and were I making a choice of a residence in India I know of no place I would prefer to it. But Ireland agrees better with me, and I shall therefore spend the rest of my days here.

I can easily see that you are anxious to clear off the mortgage, and Messrs. Jephson & Co have authority & instructions from me to sell if they can realise the value, and I am sure they will give you a preference in the matter.

There are many parts of your astonishingly witty (!) letter I have not noticed, parts of it you make me the author of "sayings & doings" which I never thought I'll take my ---- [sic].

Mrs. Moorhead joins me in kind regards to Mrs. Monk and self.

Yours sincerely,
Wm. Moorhead.

A typical market scene from the late nineteenth century with British women in palanquins carried by Indian bearers and local merchants selling their ware

LETTER XLVIII

From W. MOORHEAD, Drum, Clones, Ireland
To M. F H. MONK, Rajpore. [Extracts only]

30 APRIL 1845

"The failure of Jephson & Co is a great loss to me." He will do anything now for cash! He thought he could sell the mortgage. Has Monk heard of the mortgage being on the market? The houses on the estate are in good repair. "I would have done well in Rajpore with no more capital than you." "But I know your health failing was a great matter against you." "I hear the 'grand trunk road' from Rajpore to Mussoorie & Landour has been commenced, which will much improve [... ? ...] I town & country." Reference to Mrs. Monk & the little one. [i.e. Hugh Lewin Monk]

LETTER XLIX

From M. FITZH. MONK at ..?
To W. MOORHEAD. "No.1" [Copy]

5 MAY 1845

My Dear Moorhead,

I am quite at a loss to account for your silence, & think my letter to you of the 9th August last might have met with a reply before this. In the belief of my father's ability & willingness to assist me I then wrote offering to restore you the Victoria estate or give £700 as a balance for it. I find that I cannot do the last, and am very willing to abide by the first, if you think it worth your while to accept it. My other creditors are pressing heavily upon me for payment of their accounts, and at present I am unable to meet them. Should a docket be struck against me of which there is every probability unless I can conclude satisfactory arrangements with them, I need scarcely remind you that you will either have to rest content with your mortgage, or by foregoing that, let the estate be sold and come in with the other creditors for whatever dividend that and the rest of my effects (not worth 200 Rs, everything nearly having been sacrificed to maintain my wife and family) may bring. These arrangements I cannot make till you, who are my principle [sic] creditor, choose to give either your assent or dissent to one or other of those I am now about to propose, or substitute some other which I can in justice accept or else see some probability of being able to meet. lst proposal then, the resumption of the estate by you, giving up to me all the vouchers you hold with a receipt in full. 2nd proposal— The payment by me of £800 without interest (the addition of £100 having been made to my first offer to meet the demand for interest) in manner following, viz. the sum of £200 during each of the years 1846, 1847, 1848 and 1849. The first payment to be made previous to the 31st Dec 1846 and each succeeding one in like manner during each succeeding year to your credit in London. If made in Calcutta, the sum of 2000 Rs to be considered equivalent to £200.

The only condition that I ask is that the estate may be considered in its natural subdivisions and if the offer be accepted, a fair apportionment of the amount be made on each subdivision to enable me by the sale of the first released to release the second, and so forth. Thus, say £300 on the lower bungalow, £300 on the middle bw estate and £200 on the upper one. Such an arrangement would, were I thus empowered to sell, probabily [sic] enable me to pay off in a very short time, as I have no wish [to] retain one atom of property in so unhealthy a kennel as Rajpore.

If the above (the latter) is acceded to, I can make terms with my other creditors; and I will work night & day to do you justice as well as them, to whom it shall also be done if you resume the estate. A negative on both by you leaves me the only alternative of "getting whitewashed", and commencing life anew in India with the stock in trade I first landed in the country with, and not without some well paid experience, which cannot fail to benefit me hereafter. There is no lack of situations in Bengal, and I would sooner live as a kurasher [kuradree?] the reminder [sic] of my days than use the slightest exertion to remove a certainty a [sic] self-imposed, mountain, which must paralyse every effort I could make to benefit my family by my own exertions. I could say much more, but am pressed on this occasion for time …

Your's [sic] truly,
M. Fitzh Monk.

LETTER L

From M. FITZH. MONK, Landour
To W. MOORHEAD. "NO.2" [Copy]

4 JULY 1845

My Dear Moorhead,

This is the last safe date for the overland of the present month, & though I hasten to answer yours of the 30th April, received only yesterday, & the first & only one which has come to hand, I cannot as you may conclude by my letter of the 5th May, do so satisfactorily in this short time. The will is not wanting, but the means are, for never was I in such a state of utter destitution as I am now; nor can I accuse myself of any extravagancies which could have produced such effects. My endeavour to procure a satisfactory settlement thro' my father having failed for want of means,* I will now try amongst some monied acquaintances here, & at Meeruth, what sum they will advance me on the estate, if any, Rajpore not being now a favourite in the money market. I have tried the Himalaya Club & pointed out to them the advantages of having a stock farm, good stabling for their Arabs & buggy horses, a receiving house for the members, godowns for their palkees & tents & buggies &c, but without effect, the club being in debt. The result of all my inquiries amounts to this. No one will buy the estate as a whole, but were I able to sell in detail I could [deleted] might get Rs 6000 for the place. You have been already informed that my advertisements for a tenant or partner met with no success, & these were issued when I first found how physically I was unfitted for my work, both from the effects of climate, & my being unused to laborious outdoor work.

Your mention of the mortgage deed being in the market is the first communication I have ever had upon the subject & truly do I regret not having heard of it, for I doubt not I could have found a purchaser, who would have relieved both you & me of all future anxiety on the subject. There is one thing, however, you could no more have made a valid transfer of the mortgage bond without my consent, than I could have sold the estate without your concurrence.

Where, by the bye, are those vouchers? Before I can effect anything I must ascertain this, that is, if I succeed in getting a loan, I may be able to say in whose possession they remain. Jephson's bankruptcy was a mystery to me for months after it occurred. I hear his final examination takes place to-morrow in Calcutta.

Your hint about the stitch in time was well anticipated. Every precaution was used & an expenditure of nearly Rs 1000 incurred but such a monsoon as that of 1844 was not to be resisted by tiled houses, unless they had had a far greater slope in the roof, or tiles had been imported express from Europe for the purpose of tiling them. I would have thatched, but the Rajpore people, indignant at my innovation in importing my own grain &c would have very soon contrived a "destructive fire" to cure me of setting them at defiance. Expect a fuller letter from me next month, I trust a more satisfactory one. In the mean time I shall not be idle & you may depend upon my exertions. I don't know what may still be your opinion of the Dhoon climate, but this I feel sure of, that, constitutionally, I am ten years older than I was in 43. Bear Witness, my hoary locks!

The "Grand Trunk" Road will pass thro' Meerut & Saharunpur to Umballa, but so far are we from meeting with favour from the powers that be, that a most positive refusal of his sanction to Mr. Mackinnon's proposal for making a road to Landour & Mussoorie has been given by our new Govr General. So much for local improvements.

Mrs. Monk & her only living boy are both thriving here. She unites with me in kind regards to yourself & Mrs. Moorhead, & with best wishes for the health of your little family, Believe me,

Your's, sincerely,
M. Fitzh Monk.

*[At this point, the following had been deleted]:

"As I can do absolutely nothing of myself I write by this date to my brother in law Dr. Nicholas Magrath to communicate with you freely on the matter & I trust I may induce him to do so. Except my father, who is stricken in years & constitution, I have no male relatives in Europe whom I could get to act for me but him & if he can manage, with his large family, a loan for me, I have no doubt he will. I send him a copy of this letter of yours."

LETTER LI

From M. F. MONK, Academy, Landour
To W. MOORHEAD. "No.3" [Copy]

26 JULY 1845

My Dear Moorhead,

It appears we are now to have a bimonthly [originally: "We have notice of a bimonthly ..."] mail, & as I have not been idle since the 4th inst, when I last wrote you, I hasten this "latest safe day" to indite the sum of my exertions, enquiries, correspondences &c &c, which have all tended to one object, viz. the endeavour to meet your wishes with a sum in ready money, sufficient to make up an amount, with what has been already paid you, that will protect you from loss.

Now, as far as I can see there are two feasible ways of managing this, by either of which a sum not exceeding Rs 5000 may be obtained but, it is indispensable that all the vouchers should be in the hands of someone on the spot, to be made over, in one case, as securities, should be [sic] money be raised by loan; or to a purchaser, should one be found. By either of these means I will exert myself to raise the sum I have above mentioned if you will be satisfied with that.

You may fancy how highly the estate is valued when the invalided Quarter-Master Sergeant of Prince Albert's Own, a fellow both with brains & money, said he would give Rs 800 for the Ladies Bungalows ground but not more & I have heard many declare they would not give Rs 3000 for the whole premises, tho' they say it would be worth that if the water were brought on the estate—a thing never likely to take place in consequence of the determined opposition of the Canal Officers.

In anticipation of your answer I will advertise and see what luck I may have. I have not the slightest wish to retain any portion of property at Rajpore; for the medical men will allow neither my wife nor myself to live there. [Next sentence has been deleted.] Indeed these rains I have been laid up with the return of fever contracted by my residence in that unhealthy village. Awaiting &c &c. M. F. M.

LETTER LII

From BESSY MONK, Rajpore
To MARGARET MONK, Ann's Place, Guernsey.
Endorsed: Guernsey 12 Oct 1845.

7 AUGUST 1845

My Dear Margaret,

Your very affectionate letter of the twenty seventh May occasioned us great pain to hear of your dear father's indisposition. We trust he has quite recovered from it. Our very best thanks for the present. I shall consider it exclusively Hugh's, and Mauger intends putting it out of reach at once by laying it out to the best advantages for him. He is writing a long letter to his father and will I dare say tell him all about it, I do not quite understand the life insurance he talks about. I have been obliged to leave the hills with baby and another very sickly boy in consequence of the hooping cough breaking out at Landour but how long the doctor intends exiling us here I cannot say. Rajpore has no charms for me; and therefore the sooner he orders us up the better I shall be pleased at it though I would and will suffer any inconvenience to save Hugh from the infection. I don't think there is a disease I fear so much as the hooping cough. I have no recollection of this feeling as I had it when very young, but from what I saw one of our boys suffering, it must be a shocking complaint particularly for an infant.

Your dear father ought not to fatigue himself with any work just now—his years, and the complaint he is subject to are surely reasons sufficient for his allowing himself all excuse possible, besides, the comfort and happiness of the members of his family at home or abroad repose chiefly in his health. I know when there is any the thing the matter with him we are very uneasy and if anything were to happen to him it would be a source of the greatest unhappiness to us particularly to Mauger who I believe would do very much to see him again, so I hope he will take care of himself for his children's sake. You give me a very unfavourable opinion of the winters in Guernsey for I assure you it is quite bad enough to have it here till March though the most unpleasant part of our year is the monsoon. The fogs and rain then are constant from the middle of June nearly to the end of September. The thunder and lightening are most frightful sometimes. The other night a rock not above a few yards away from the house we live in at Landour, was struck by it and I hear the shock was very severe.

It is very warm down here, though not unpleasantly so. The change agrees extremely well with baby, he continues well thank God and has not commenced teething yet. He will be nine months old on the thirteenth of this month.

Mauger had an attack of fever but is now quite well. Dear father said he was afraid about his going out shooting, his occupation seldom allows him time, nor, do I think he has so great an inclination for it now as he had. He has also entirely left of [sic] spirits and we keep but little wine in the house, in the use of which he is very moderate. We have at last heard from Mr. Moorehead and not so unfavourably as was expected. The man seems eager to come to any reasonable terms. Love to my dear sisters, kisses to Sarah's children and my kindest love to dear father and with prayers for his health believe me

Your very affectionate sister,
Elizabeth Monk.

[From MAUGER]

P.S. Bess, sent me this from Rajpore about dak time. You may read it if you can—I can't—but mind she has no bone in the first joint of her thumb. It was taken out for Whitlow, & she behaved nobly. love & kisses. My Dearest Sarah, Shall I make more kisses? Tell Mugra, as the natives wod say, to fit his boys for the Indian market, as sawbones. It is the best trade going. Love to all from Uncle Mauger. Tell Nick-nix Gun-nix Arab-nix Dukhanee-nix Grog-nix indulgence of any kind for the last six months.

LETTER LIII

From M. F. MONK Landour
To Geo. JEPHSON Calcutta. [Copy]

19 OCTOBER 1845

My Dear Sir,

I have the pleasure to acknowledge the receipt of your two letters, resply [sic] of the 9th instant, & in replying, first, to that which relates to the affairs of Mr. Wm. Moorhead, to explain conduct, which to you appears more than suspicious & which you have pronounced 'illegal'. The following explanation will, I think, remove any grounds for mistrust or suspicion but I am sufficiently well acquainted with the law of tenure to know that as respects the mortgagee (Moorhead) I might have sold the place fifty times over without his claim on the estate being in the slightest degree prejudiced. His lien would, for years, have been as good as ever; the victim of the fraud would have been the purchaser, who could only have sought redress from me. The advertisement you allude to, as well as a former one were inserted with the best views, that of finding out who were inclined to treat for the estate or parts of it & of my intention to advertise, more for his benefit than mine, Moorhead was duly informed before I ever wrote to the gazette office.

With a registered mortgage & without a single title deed to produce, it was morally impossible for me alone to dispose of the place for who would have been fool enough to buy it? The fact of

Moorhead's being the mortgagee (a pretty notorious circumstance in these parts of the country!) must have become known to any intending purchasers, who had used the common precaution of looking into the register; & had any one then bought with his eyes open, no British law would have ever protected him against the mortgagee's claim. He "had had ample notice", as the law terms it. I have been thus diffuse in my exordium, as your anxiety for your client has most probably led you to convey an erroneous opinion to the Superintend[an]t of the Dhoon of the honesty of my intentions with regard to the Victoria, & to make him believe that he has a rogue within his jurisdiction whom he did not previously suspect to be so. I shall by to-day's post order the advertisement to be discontinued.

To the foreclosing of the mortgage I shall not offer the slightest opposition. Indeed, I do not see what else you as Moorhead's attorney can do, unless you act against me. The law certainly leaves you this alternative on foregoing the mortgage when I am sure my other creditors will immediately pounce on the estate, which is the only thing I should have to satisfy them with; for my personals, which have been gradually diminishing to keep my family & myself from starving, would scarcely realise Rs 300. To no others but my wife & myself are they even worth that; & even these must have been sacrificed for what they would have fetched, but for the timely aid afforded me by about £70, the share of my poor brother's China prize money which fell to my lot, as well as for the kindness of a benevolent gentleman here, who has assisted me with loans; for the little school I tried to establish here has not averaged more than eight pupils per mensem since May last.

I date my ruin from the time of taking the hotel. Just before I did so, in May 1843, I was worth between 6000 & 8000 Rs in cash;- before the lst January 1845 I was not only the last amount in debt, in addition to the mortgage, (for every penny I had, had been sunk in the Victoria) but I had lost my first born, my wife nearly followed, & my own health had become so impaired as to be refused the risk of an insurance on it. So late as last month the Church of England Assurance Office in Calcutta declined the risk, upon what grounds I know not.

So long as my own strength & health remained. I managed tolerably well & had the promissory note due in Nov 1843 been presented about that time, I could have paid great part of it, & borrowed or given security for the remainder. Finding nothing was said about it, I laid out what I had collected in building a new godown & in improving the estate generally. Rs 1,000 (the receipt of which, by the bye. has never been acknowledged) I remitted to you on account in Jany 1844.

To the above I have to add, that all hopes & expectations I may hitherto have formed of assistance from home, have been most unceremoniously destroyed by my father's declaration that I can never expect another 6 D from him.

I have now fully explained how I stand with Moorhead & with the world generally. It is for you to act as you think most advisable for your principal's interest. I cannot, however, close this letter without pointing out that beggared as I am beyond redemption after having expended all I possessed on the Victoria, the mortgagee on quietly foreclosing the mortgage & resuming the estate can afford to be somewhat generous. For myself I ask nothing & he could well spare my boy the old thatched bungalow he bought of Messrs Scott & Co. for Rs 1200 & which has never formed part of the hotel estate. This would at least serve as a shelter for my wife & child; & given to the latter, it could not be touched for my liabilities.

I am quite as anxious as you are to do justice to Moorhead, and shall indeed be most happy to have this business amicably adjusted in time.

Hoping to hear from you soon & trusting your own matters have been wound up to your satisfaction, believe me to be, my dear sir,

Your's, very faithfully,
M. Fitzh. Monk.

P.S. If the mortgage is foreclosed, I should like to be furnished with an attested copy of the power of attorney & its transfer—if one be made.

To M.F.MONK.

Receipt for payments for advertising the sale of Victoria Hotel & the best bungalow on the Victoria Estate at Rajpore.

Annus Horribilis 1846

LETTER LIV

From M. F. MONK, Landour
To W. MOORHEAD. [Copy]

3 JANUARY 1846

My Dear Moorhead,

I am, I regret to say, in no situation to accept your offer. The only thing I can do is to repeat my previous one of Rs 8,000 payable in four years, in full of all demands upon me, direct or indirect, and if this is accepted, I will add a policy of insurance on my life as a collateral security, to the promissory notes of Rs 2,000 each, payable respectively without interest the 31st Dec 1846, 47, 48 and 49 to any one, whom you may appoint here as the holder. The estate is in no better condition than when you purchased it, & I honestly assure you, it would not, in my belief, realise Rs 5,000 if offered for sale. In deciding upon this offer, the best with any certainty of paying it I can make, I must request you to use no unnecessary delay, as well as your answering either in the negative or the affirmative.

If you accept, appoint at once an agent either here or at Mussoorie, that I may be put in a situation to realise, with his consent, by sale of part of the property sufficient to meet my first note, any surplus being devoted to the putting & sustaining the rest of the property into good repair & a saleable condition. I am without a sixpence in the world, & at present my income derived from a very few pupils falls short of my expenditure, so that you see without some arrangement of this kind, I am unable to repair the premises which are daily deteriorating. If you decline, I am prepared for the worst, & fully resolved, though with deep pain & regret, to clear myself of my encumbrances by application to the Insolvent Debtors Court. It is not my wish to benefit in the least by my proposed arrangement but to ensure you full payment, if possible from the estate, of the sum I have offered. I cannot but conclude with expressing my deep regret at the untoward circumstances which have led to my entire impoverishment & the loss & trouble you have been put to,

Yrs snc'y
M. F. M.

[On reverse:]

Victoria Hotel, Rajpore. *SUN*, a new novel, more "*Tales of my Landlord*", or *The Himalayan Victoria.* Apply for specimens not to Thacker & Co. Publishers but on the spot to the proprietor, M. F. Monk.

LETTER LV

From BESSY MONK, Rajpore

To SARAH MAGRATH, Manor House, St.Peter Port, Guernsey.

Endorsed: Guernsey, 10 Apr 1846.

16 FEBRUARY 1846

My Dear Sister,

In vain have we looked for a letter from home for the last three months, every mail disappointed us. I trust you are all well; for although I know your father is vexed with Mauger, I think Isabella or Margaret would have written if nothing else had occured [sic]. Here we hear little else besides "glorious victory" and "dreadful slaughter" and you who are so far from can little imagine what a sensation this news creates. I expect our hills will be crowded by ladies from all stations, for the Simla hills are too close to the Punjaub to be visited this year. I trust this expedition will end well for the horrors of the Cabul campaign are still fresh in our memories.

Hugh continues well thank God, he has cut eight teeth without any ailments ... Mauger received a letter from William last Dec. I wonder if he will ever visit us; he talks of it. I hope Papa is satisfied with Mauger's explanation of Moorhead's affair, and that he will now accept our love. Also kindly give my love to Isabella and Margaret and to your dear children and their Papa.

Your very affectionate sister,

E.Monk.

LETTER LVI

From BESSY MONK, 'Elseworth', Landour
To ISABELLA MONK, Ann's Place, Guernsey, Channel Isles.
"Per Overland Mail via Southamp ton."
[Stamped:] "AL 28 MY 28 1846" "Guernsey May 29 1846"

1 APRIL 1846

My Dear Isabella,

Your letter of the twelfth of January, lately received, was truly welcome, for it is more than four months since we had a letter from any one at home and your last having given an unfavourable account of your father's health we were rather anxious about him, however, thank God, he is quite well again, but it gives Mauger great pain to hear of his old nurse's ill health, and although I do not know her personally her affection has been so often expressed towards Mauger in your letters that I also feel quite sad about her. The china figures she sent for my boy have not been given to him to break but he is occasionally allowed to take them down from their usual standing place, the mantle piece and kiss them which he is very fond of doing. When he is older and can understand it, he shall be told who sent them for him and if no unforeseen accident destroys them, they shall be kept as a memorial of the good old woman's affection towards Mauger and his children. We are all well, thank God, and doing pretty well with the school. We have many promises & the good wishes of many; so I have not the least doubt of Mauger's having quite as much to do as he can manage, himself, for no other assistance than soldiers either from the depot here or from stations in the plains can be had in Upper India, and of these he has seen so much, and, to my knowledge, we lost so much by them in our last business that Mauger is determined to have nothing to do with any of them again. He has limited the school to thirty boarders. As I am rather pressed for time from nursing and other household affairs you will I am sure excuse the shortness of this letter. With love to our dear father, Margaret & Sarah and her dear children believe me, my dear sister,

Yours very affectionately,
E. Monk.

LETTER LVII

From MAUGER MONK, Landour Academy
To HUGH MONK Esq. R.N., Ann's Place, Guernsey.

3 MAY 1846

My Dear Father,

The announcement in my brother William's letter of the lst March that I had become entitled to any thing by poor Uncle William's decease surprised me more than the intimation that you had, with your usual kindness, increased the amount to £100. You will, I trust, believe me sincere in my gratitude for this unlooked for bounty, which the rate of exchange being high I have drawn for, the amount Rs 1089, being to credited, when realised, to my interest account with the North Western Bank of India. The bank allows me 6 per cent on my deposit, subject to 6 months notice of withdrawal, & this, in the event of my only creditor having recourse to unpleasant measures, is my reserve fund for my wife & child, children, I may almost say; as a few months will, under God's blessing, see a second born to us. Should he not come into terms, I made arrangements for the care of my family with my wife's father, & my brother-in-law will, pro tempore, take charge of my school, which is getting on well. I have 15 boarders at £40 per annum, one day boarder & 10 day scholars, 4 of whom learn drawing.

I have every encouragement & shall by the end of the year complete my numbers; some of the day scholars remain as boarders when their parents return to the plains, and the younger brothers of some of my present pupils are to come to me next year.

My dear little wife, who is of course ailing, unites with me in kindest love to you, & our sisters. Little Hugh, who has commenced to walk, or rather, toddle alone is very like his poor uncle after whom he was named, and to judge from those I see around me, more intelligent than the generality of Indo-European children. With hooping cough raging around us, we have hitherto been most fortunate in escaping any visitation this season. The effects of the late frightful war are visible in the nos of lame, blind & otherwise mutilated officers and soldiers we meet in our daily walks, all sent up to this beautiful climate to be cured & get convalescent.

Give my best love & kisses to Sarah's dear boys & little Ellen, as well as to Uncle Joseph & Aunt Eliza, & do not forget to remember me most kindly to my good old nurse. With sincere prayers for your health, believe me to be, my dear father,

Your ever affectionate son,
Mauger Fitzh Monk.

LETTER LVIII

From BESSY MONK, Landour
To HANNAH LEWIN, Meeruth.

2 JUNE 1846

My Dearest Hannah,

I am truly sorry to hear of Isaac's having only 10 pupils. This must make your income very small but tell me my dear Hannah if it is sufficient for your wants and do not feel hurt at the question for you must place as much confidence in me in writing as you used in conversation for I have been quite unhappy. We are all well again thank God but I hear there is much sickness among the children at Mussoorie ... G ... [?] Huish buried twins in one grave a couple of evenings ago. I write to you before that Mrs. Moorhouse is married to a Mr. Gurney, tailor, at Nunballa[?]. We had a very nice letter of thanks from her saying she could not think of leaving Kit on our hands now that she could maintain him, but we shall keep him till October and then send him home by the first opportunity. Poor Mr. Healy is going fast, there is little hope of his recovery. I am happy to say Mr. Boys performed morning service at Landour not from any orders but of his wish to lighten Mr. Brooke's duties particularly as the old man has been laid up for three weeks with influenza. He is quite well now. With love to papa and Isaac, believe me,

Your very affecte sister,
E. Monk.

LETTER LIX

From MAUGER FITZHUGH MONK, Landour
To HANNAH LEWIN.

3 JUNE 1846

My Dearest Hannah,

Many thanks for your most comme il faut letter, which desrves and shall have a separate reply, possibly on Saturday, if fine certainly if raining as it is almost sure to be.

There is some luck for the Nash family in housing near the shadow of our roof. Two of Coll Nash's daughters, living where Capt Trower did last year, just under us, are, I hear, both engaged. I can't say when they are to be married though. The elder is pretty, very pleasing and loveable. The younger very pretty & lovely & I dare say loving enough too. I can add naught to the news Bess has given except that she gets into a fright occasionally at the thunder & lightning, tho' we have had none to alarm us except one night when some outhouses at Mussoorie were struck & then she slept through it all.

Give love to Isaac & tell him I have a rather handsome ship's barometer for him with thermometer attached, but he will have to fill the tube himself. I'll tell him more about it on Saturday but as I have a mountain barometer to fill also and no access to an encyclopaedia, he must for his own information & mine get hold of Mrs. Gregg's, and find out how the tubes are cleansed, the mercury defecated, & tell me what I can't understand how the air gets into the cup containing the superfluous mercury, as the vessel is closed, & consequently how the barometer acts. More next time. Busses from self & Hugh to Aunty 'no' Dear, he never says t'other & with best love to Papa, believe me

Your's ever affectionately
M. Fitzh Monk.

Traveling across the hilly terrain was made easy with the construction of roads and introduction of motor vehicles

LETTER LX

From M. F. MONK, Landour
To W. MOORHEAD. [Copy]

26 JULY 1846

My Dear Moorhead,

It has only very lately struck me as most probable that the original of the subjoined letter was lost in the *Great Liverpool*, having on board at the time she was wrecked the Bombay Mail of the 15th Jan. I can only add that in the event of my offer being accepted, I am likely to be a still greater loser, for there is scarcely an outhouse remaining on the estate & part of the roof of the Bachelor's Bungalow has fallen in. Instead, however, of the 31st Decr 1846, 1847, 1848 & 1849 you must read lst July 1847, 1848, 1849 & 1850, or it will not be in my power to meet my engagements. I fully rely on getting your reply early in Decr; should it be unsatisfactory, I have but the option of the court or quitting the country. On one of the two I am fully resolved, for I have no notion of eking out much longer a beggarly existence in the instruction of some six or eight children. I can say, however, that since I was compelled to give up business, I have not received a pice from the estate. The little that has come in, by way of rent, has been insufficient to keep the whole in repair. Looking anxiously for a reply in Decr, I remain,

Your's truly,
M. Fitzh. Monk.

LETTER LXI

From BESSY MONK, Elseworth, Landour
To SARAH MAGRATH, Manor House, Guernsey.
Endorsed: 2 Nov 1846 [Guernsey?]
[Bessy died on 21 Sept 1846]

25 AUGUST 1846

My Dear Sister,

I am almost tempted to leave my letter till next mail as Mauger is writing to Isabella, but if I do so most probably I shall then be laid up, and I should have a fresh excuse for gratifying my idle vein a month or two longer; we, Indian borns understand the feeling of the "dolce far niente", &c, there is a dear sister, be charitably inclined when you receive this and make some allowance for its faults, as I am not in the humour for letter writing. You could not have sent me a more pleasing letter than your last, for I have wished much to know all about my nephews and niece; I had no idea they were such grown up boys. How many of them are inclined to follow their father's proffession [sic]? Mauger has taken it into his head that one of them should be a parson, come out to India, first obtaining the perpetual Chaplaincy of Landour, (some £600 a year under the new regulations) bring out a nice, dear little wife with him, and become the nominal head of what he seems determined to make an incipient college. I believe he would himself give a trifle to be able to sign himself B.A. or M.A. and worlds to be a D.D. He does jestingly subscribe himself "A.J.S.

(that I have been)," to which of course, I suggest his adding the present tense as well. He has another embryo scheme for William, who he, yankee like, calculates will at the expiration of the charter some eight years hence, be tired of the sea, and be willing to accept the house surgeonry of our noble hospital. There never yet has been a resident surgeon, nor under the Company will one ever be appointed, as he says; therefore, he thinks when the British government take matters into their own hands, a little interest with the board of control could redily [sic] secure an appointment in the mountains, so far removed from Calcutta as we are. As I know nothing of these matters I merely listen, but I agree with him in thinking that the private practice would pay handsomely. We have had upwards of five hundred badly wounded men and officers here this season and with only two assistant surgeons to attend them. These two have found plenty of time to see their patients and one of them to go to all parties and balls besides. One doctor, the quiet one, is a very good man, a great patron of Mauger's, and exceedingly attentive. With the other I don't know how many times he has quarrelled. He is, I believe, a West Indian, very proud, and very hasty-tempered. Mauger calls him "that Creole brute".

I wish I could tell you all about my dear little "monkey", who is getting too strong for me, and about whom I believe enough has already been said. My anxieties are, as you may imagine, about the coming one, especially as I have one to care for, and am constantly haunted with all sorts of fears, which seem to be the burden of my nightly dreams. It is foolish, I allow but, though I strive against it, anxiety will be uppermost. In one of our evening candle conversations, I suggested, should the little one prove a girl to call her "Sarah", a most unfortunate name for me to light upon, up here, as at Rajpore, we are surrounded by them, and my liege Lord wished to know if it was to be Sarah the twenty-fifth or the thirty-fifth, and expressed an intention of making the boy, should it so turn out, Abraham. You see we have been reckoning chickens prematurely, at last I coaxed him into good humour and Lawrence Magrath or Isabella Elizabeth, as the case may be; the latter, I think, a sort of union of myself and Aunt Eliza, were finally settled by his lordship.

He has promised to give a full account of ourselves to Isabella, and as he can, when he chooses, write a long letter, I must depend on him, for, truth to say, in addition to my laziness I cannot sit any length of time. Love and kisses to all at Ann's place and all aunts and uncles. My most affectionate love to my nephews and niece and believe me my dear sister to remain,

Your very affectionate sister,
Elizabeth Monk.

LETTER LXII

From MAUGER MONK, 'Elseworth', Landour
To Dr. NICHOLAS MAGRATH, Guernsey.

25 SEPTEMBER 1846

My Dear Nicholas,

It pleased Almighty God to give me early on the morning of the 10th a fine little daughter, but it was his will also that my dear darling Bess should no longer remain a tenant of this world. Poor, poor girl, fusion of the brain with low fever carried her off at the early age of twenty four, the eleventh day after her confinement. She had for some time been subject to hysteria, and the severity of the season (the monsoon) combined with her weakness, are supposed to have hastened, if not induced, the catastrophe. There was not an officer in the station with whom we had the slightest acquaintance, absent from her funeral, and she was borne to the grave by twenty volunteers from the artillery. Oh! How truly desolate is my once cheerful home. The boys have all been taken away to different friends' houses and my two poor children were walked off to the Commandant's house by his lady almost without asking my consent, and here am I alone half beside myself, and but for my poor bairns' sake utterly reckless of the future. On the 28th I shall re-open the school again in hope that employment will prevent my becoming what I nearly am now, mad. It only requires that scoundrel Moorhead to throw me into jail to give a climax to my misery. What I am to do with my little girl requires serious consideration, and that I cannot now give the subject; tho' the lady, who has her, returns to Europe in a few days. Some active friends are trying to engage a good old housekeeper for me, and I trust they may succeed, for without a manager in the domestic department, the school, which is now thriving, will go on badly—the Mussulman servants in the kitchen rob one so unblushingly, and of late we have had no power to flog them as we used to do. I flogged my grain-keeper for mixing pulse with the peas, and was fined £5 (50 Rupees) with a promise of the full penalty £50 (500 Rupees) the next time it occurred. I can write no more now, my dear Nicholas, but give my best love to my poor father, Sarah and her dear boys—Magrath major in particular—dear Bell, Margaret & William and give one tear of sympathy to

Your affectionate, but heart-broken brother,
M. Fitzh. Monk.

LETTER LXIII

From W. MOORHEAD, 6 Bachelor's Walk, Dublin
To M. F. MONK, Landour.

30 SEPTEMBER 1846

Moorhead is pressed for cash. "It looks strange that you should now after a lapse of 31/2 years* without having paid a rupee of interest or principal make such an offer." Recriminations from Moorhead. He thinks Monk has let him down over the management of the estate and maintenance of the houses. "I was pleased to hear from Meerut that you were doing well at Landour."

* [Marginal note by Monk:]
"Hypocrite! It was made to him two years ago or more."

LETTER LXIX

From MAUGER MONK, Elseworth, Landour
To HUGH MONK Esq., R.N., Ann's Place, Guernsey.
Endorsed: 11 Jan 1847 [Guernsey?].
[H M had died on 3 Dec 1846.]

6 NOVEMBER 1846

My Dearest Father,

This is probably the last letter I shall write you from this house, which I quit on the 28th for my winter residence at the foot of the hills, and as I could not live here again, I shall as soon as my brother-in-law joins me as my partner, select a good house & rent it for a term. Since the season closed & the families belonging to the civil & military services left this station for the plains, & the long nights have set in I have been subject to fearful fits of despondency consequent on the low nervous fever, which attacked me shortly after my beloved's demise; but thro' God's mercy, the bracing air & the attention of the doctors I am nearly well again. My school thrives apace and though I have for the winter but fourteen or fifteen resident pupils, I calculate on opening in the spring, the first of the season, with more than double that number & a score of day-scholars so that I see nothing to prevent. My two dear children, my beautiful babes, are, thank Heaven, strong, healthy & good tempered. Hugh is a noble little fellow, chattering all the morning to his "Pap-pa" a mixture of English & Hindostanee. He was two years old three days ago (the 13th). The little baby, whom

I have christened "Elizabeth Isabella", is a real cherub. For her I procured, at a heavy cost certainly, a young, healthy high-caste (Indian prejudices, heh! Master Mauger?) wet-nurse, and it is truly surprising how much she has thriven since. She is a little picture.

Had I time to spare from my avocations I would delight your heart with copies of some of the testimonials voluntarily furnished to me by parents, whose children I have educated and am still educating. The proudest address me as "My dear Sir", the generality as "My dear Mr Monk" & as a proof of public confidence, our dear old clergyman, the Revd Mr. Brooke, who examines the pupils, is so dissatisfied with the progress his three boys have made at home that they are now on their way out in the Earl of Hardwicke to be educated by me under his own eye. This is not written as a brag, but to show you that I am getting on in the world. With fondest love & kisses to my dear sisters, brother, Magrath, nephews, nieces, aunts, uncle & all my nearest relatives, & kind regards to any inquiring friends, I remain, my dearest father,

Your unfortunate & afflicted
but still dutiful & affectionate son,
M. Fitzh Monk.

P.S. Not having heard from any of you this long time I judge from the papers dear Sarah sends me that you are well. God spare you to us these many years to come, my dearest father & a cheerful Christmas & happy new year to you all.

A NEW START
1848

LETTER LXX

From MAUGER MONK, Constantia, Rajpore
To NICHOLAS MAGRATH, Manor House, Guernsey.
Endorsed: Guernsey 2 March 1848.

3 JANUARY 1848

My Dear Magrath,

Here I am with a few pupils wintering in the Dhoon or valley of Dhera, and just convalescent from a nasty low fever, brought on by what you'd call my "puling". Give the cause what name you like, I have had affliction enough to try me sorely, and though now well, & I trust, a different man, I have had a very narrow escape, and am told that I look full fifty years of age. On reference to my letter-receipt book I find I wrote to you on the 31st Augt & tho' most of the events of the past year are to me a perfect blank, I have some vague idea that that letter contained both an explanation & an apology (though I had been completely misled) and I trust that these were satisfactory. Being in the habit of destroying private letters as soon as I have read them, I have none to refer to, & perhaps, it is better as it is, for the chances are I shod be worrying myself about things that are past. As a month has elapsed since the time appointed for winding up the affairs, there is most likely a letter for me en route, which I shall gladly welcome, my late illness being a hint to me that I shod set my house in order, and, whilst hoping for the best, be prepared for the worst. To add to my troubles I have this winter a return of a complaint, wh first shewed itself in the winter of 1845 and then attacked me in the left wrist—rheumatic gout. It was cured by the application of leeches & iodine ointment. This second touch is in the left knee, wh is so painful that I cannot bend it. Our doctor, the Landour one, in attempting to throw himself from a runaway horse, turned his leg and tore the ligamt below the knee cap nearly thro. Doctor, No. 2, at Mussoorie, broke his leg on Friday the 30th, his horse falling on him, when going to see a patient, the fashionable school-mistress, old Mrs.Cowan, who had tumbled down stairs and sustained a compound fracture of the ancle-bone. Doctor, No. 3, has the other two to nurse, the body-guard & a battalion of rifles, the former corps with the Dhoon fever amongst them & the latter (all Ghoorkas) with the small-pox, besides a full station at Deyrah. If No. 3 does his work, he ought to sleep in his saddle. In the season we have no less than seven spare sawbones, all visiting the hills on sick certificate. Excuse the brevity of this. For the last week I have been at work for ten hours a day, bringing up arrears of accounts & correspondence. With best love to all & wishing you, Sarah, the boys & Ellen many very happy returns of the new year, I remain,

Your's affectionately,
M. Fitzh Monk.

When you write address, Landour, Bengal. Only wintering here.

LETTER LXXI

Quotation from Alliance Insurance, Meerut for a life policy of 10,000 Rs. on M. F. Monk.
69. 1 April 1848. From MAUGER MONK, Mullingar House, Landour
To MARGARET MONK, c/o Joseph Mauger Esq,
Esplanade, Guernsey.
Endorsed: Guernsey 28[?] May 1848.

27 JANUARY 1848

My Dear Margaret,

Don't imagine from the date of my letter that I am going to play "Poisson d'Avril" with you, though I am going to give you a bit of a scolding for not writing oftener to me, seeing that you cannot have much to do, nor many cares to trouble you. I have half a mind to send Hugh home to keep you in mind of his papa and to give you—you, Madge, in particular, plenty to do to keep him out of mischief. Luckily, probably, for your peace & quiet he is not only a very well behaved child, but Papa could not spare his only darling. 'Twould be too much to be left absolutely alone in the Himalaya, poor Bess & her two other babes lying in the cold, cold grave. You should, like a kind sister, write oftener to me. Your and dear Isabella's letters are but too welcome to your poor brother, who often thinks of the home he should like to, but may never see again & though he is seldom, if ever, idle; yet there are such things as fits of melancholy, periods of low spirits & sleepless nights, during wh last I love to indulge in waking visions of days

I thought I should not dare recal [sic] again, though their "bright & blameless joys" exist no longer, save in imagination.

The school goes on much the same as it did last year, without the increase I anticipated. Other schools have sprung up in the various hill-stations, & children are now generally sent to the nearest available seminary. It would be useless to grumble at fortune, were I disposed, which I am not, to do so. We have enough & to spare, and I am very contented with everything about me. Could I hear oftener of & from you, and be rid of that feeling of mental desolation, which is my bane, I could say I was happy too; for without any approach to what the world sneeringly terms being "good" (how I wish that I were!) I have sufficient Christian feeling to be thankful to the Almighty for all his mercies & bounties, aye, even for the afflictions, with which he has been pleased to visit me.

After a very mild winter, we have now a beautiful summer, for with us there is no such thing as spring, & my school-house and other works, are progressing as rapidly as work can be got to do in the mountains. The rains set in about the middle of June, when we are obliged to stop for a time here, where it absolutely pours; so you may imagine that I urge the niggers to their utmost speed.

My darling boy sends love & kisses to his aunties, & wishes to know if they are the same "aunts" he mentions in his prayers. The dear little fellow is quite well.

It will afford me great happiness to hear in your next, for I expect a letter by return of post, that you, & Isabella and the folks at Manor House are again reconciled. I never hear from them, tho' anxious to obtain from Magrath the accounts, wh are to shew me how I stand.

I have but little time to spare, so give my kindest love & kisses to Isabella, uncle & aunts, & remembrances to all inquiring friends, not omitting my best love to William when you write, & believe me to be, ever,

Your affectionate brother,
M. Fitzh Monk.

P.S. My letter concludes very abruptly. Interruptions by visitors to the school are constant, and I unfortunately deferred writing to you till the llth hour.

LETTER LXXII

From NICHOLAS MAGRATH, Guernsey
To MAUGER MONK, Landour.
Endorsed: Bombay 6 May 1848 [sic].
Letter has been added to statements of account from Mallet frères & M. Le Mesurier.

1 APRIL 1848

My Dear Mauger,

I have not much room, and in paucis verbis I shall tell you how you ought to act, & how you must act, if you intend me to have anything to do with your affairs in Europe. As to your statement of not knowing what has past in the last year, I do not believe a word of it. You have drawn your bills, you say for £850, when your £1000 consols only sold for £830, of which you mention nothing. I shall write to-night to Messrs Drummond for your acct & forward by next packet, when you will see what amount you may be able to draw for, as you will also see in this letter the amount of your balance in the Mallets' hands which they have kindly remitted at my request for safety to Drummonds. Now as the Drummonds have no dividends further[?] to receive you cannot expect them to act as agents or bankers, they being only paid by the deposit in their hands, you will see the necessity of only drawing for the exact amount in their hands, and afterwards arranging with me or the Mallets in Paris how you are to draw for your French dividends. The best manner I can suggest is that you write to them to place them at my disposal and I will arrange for them as my own, and let you know when I have recd them what am[oun]t you are to draw for, this I mention thus circumstantially as the Drummonds will not honour any further drafts from any of the family except on their own sole resposibility by the directions of the executors—the next point I have to advert to is your books & the portion of your late father's wearing apparel, the books are not worth sending to you. However as Wm's House is now empty I shall have them removed down to us, to save them from damp, and will do what you direct with your father's watch, it is now in Lemesurier's possession, whose acct you herewith receive and after the division of the property belonging to your mother in Uncle Joe's hands, I see no necessity for his further increasing your expence. The rest of the family accounts I shall also send you, altho' it is so cumbersome an abstract that the postage will be high, still it will explain the whole family affairs to you—better than I can by letter.

Wm is in the West Indies, all well I heard from him yesterday, of the girls I neither know, see or wish to know anything further of them. As I have been more than disgusted at their recent conduct, Wm is dividing the quarters (20 wheat rent) instead of taking 2/3rds as he in law was entitled to, he very liberally divided them equally, giving to each sister £88 instead of £44 or somewhat less, which they quietly pocketed, but when the balance in the executors hands came to be divided they insisted that the March/47/ Dividends in the French funds should be divided according to the stock which gave them about sixteen pounds more than honestly they ought to have had from their brothers liberality which they quietly pocketed, ergo I know them not. Next as to the division of your mothers real property, how will you divide it—equally or according to law.

Give me explicit directions, and no rhodomontade nonsense, about your not knowing what you are or have been about or not. If a man know not what he is about, he is only fit for St. Lukes, so pray never make so unmanly an excuse to me, you will have seen by the papers the fearful times we are in, I don't expect any more French dividends for years, but it would be madness to sell at so low a rate, I therefore intend to reinvest the dividends, and would recommend you to do the same, & with love & with blessings &c to you & your child believe me always

Yours sincerely affte
Br. N. Magrath.

Write to me for return of post all your plans & directions, I shall pay Le Mesurier his balance and take his final rec[eipt?] should Uncle Joe move before I hear again from you. Adieu. N M.

LETTER LXXIII

From MAUGER MONK, Landour

To NICHOLAS MAGRATH, Manor House, Guernsey.

Endorsed: Gu 1 Aug 1848.

4 JUNE 1848

My Dear Magrath,

I am much obliged to you for all the trouble you have taken on my account, & sorry you shod have disbelieved my account of myself, which, however, there is a medical man at home now, who would readily confirm. I was not exactly fitted for St. Luke's, but change of scene &c would have effected what time with little of the doctor's aid has done at last. It is no use alluding to by-gones, so I will merely say what is necessary as regards the affairs as they stand; and first as respects my French dividends. As soon as I have finished this, I will concoct as intelligible a French letter as I can to Messieurs Mallet, desiring them to place my dividends at your disposal, not that in the present state of La Belle France I imagine there will be any forthcoming for years, but I live in hopes that when the canaille-mania has abated or been made to abate & France has something like a responsible government, she will be honest enough to pay her creditors their principal, if not their arrears of dividends.

With respect to Drummond & Co I shall do as you direct on receiving their account. This is, I conjecture, en route & not far off, for the mail of the 24th April has reached us, but as yet the government express only has come in, bringing in, I am sorry to see, but a very unfavourable account of the French funds, wh were at 54-60. The heavy portion cannot be in for two or three days, though possibly some letters may reach tonight. If mine arrive I will venture on another letter to-morrow, though this (the 4th) is distinctly given out as the latest safe date for the mail, wh leaves Bombay on the 19th, should such letter require a reply. I shall be anxious to get D's account, for Mallet's commercial French is very nearly Chinese to me, and I really cannot make out what "semestre" the dividends have been paid into the London Bankers' hands, whether they are up to the "22 Mars 1848" or only those of "7bre 1847." Though the account shews the latter & the epistle states the former I do not suppose it signifies much. 'Twill all come right in the end.

You have my full consent to divide on my behalf my mother's property "equally" though in my utter ignorance of the law of the "Grand Coutumier", I should have supposed the decision of this point rested solely with William as heir-at-law. I can form no notion of what my mother's property is, never whilst at home having heard any nearer allusion to it than "Uncle Joe's accounts"; and the wheat "rentes" are almost as a great a mystery [sic]. These last have, I take it, been sold out and out, & the £88 credited in my account are my quota of what they produced. Kindly let me know some day if this surmise is correct, & enlighten me at your leisure with respect to the former. I would ask too if the transfer of the French stock has been effected and in whose name it now stands, whether mine, mine & Hugh's, or your's with mine & Hugh's. This I wish to know for my own guidance in putting my affairs here in order, should anything befal me. If I live, the chances are I marry again; for much as I loved, & respect the memory of my dear Bess, I am not bound to lead, as I must otherwise do, the life of a miserable, half-hipped recluse. Besides, my business, which is respectable & flourishing, demands the assistance of a helpmate, twelve out of my twenty-five boarders being under seven years of age & who can look after their little wants & wishes like a woman?

With regard to the books, please get rid of them if they are of no service to me. Should there be any really valuable books of reference, or a good collection of voyages & travels, put them by for me, please. I have an encyclopedia in three vols similar to the one that was in my father's library, given me by my old friend, the Revd Mr. Brooke, on leaving the station, so shod that have fallen to my lot, I do not require it. However, kindly do with them as you may think best. Wearing apparel I do not of course require; but the watch I should like to have put into good order, & sent out "overland". It will be a relic I shall dearly prize. Give my kindest love & kisses to Sarah & her bairns, & shew me that we are as we have been before by sending me the Illd *London News* again. And now, Adieu. [etc]

P.S. Since writing the above I have finished a letter to Messrs Mallet, placing the dividends at yr disposal. I wrote in English to be intelligible as they must have someone in the bank who will understand it, & no man can be sure of his interpretation of Doggrel French.

LETTER LXXIV

From MAUGER MQNK, Mullingar House, Landour
To NICHOLAS MAGRATH, Manor House, Guernsey.

5 JUNE 1848

My Dear Magrath,

I forgot in my letter of yesterday, written amid a host of interruptions, to ask a favour of you, namely, (if not too late) to collect for me as many drawings in water-colours sepia & Indian ink or body-colours, either of Young's, Coll Smith's, or any other artists, as may have escaped destruction and may not be useful or necessary at Manor House. I do not mention pencil drawings, knowing myself to be first-rate in that line. The late Surveyor-Genl of India, Coll Everest, now in Wales, said I was the best & correctest sketcher in India, so don't think the above a piece of conceit, as he has seen me at work, & did not pay me the compliment to my face. The drawings will be to me invaluable, and wherever you can get them, you may swop books, or anything else useless to me for them; indeed, when I am out of your debt; pecuniarily, for I must be long under many obligations to you and you have funds of mine in hand you may be guilty of a little extravagance for water-colour drawings, or sketches in Indian ink, Sepia or neutral tint. My style, wh once was Young's, is spoiled & I have become both finnikin & tedious in the use of a brush. Nothing of mine looks well, unless highly finished, & a tedious style is a bad one to teach. Besides, the parents of my pupils look for variety. Every boy I turn out draws as like the other as two peas.

When, or rather I should say, if the French do not stop payment, get the best of the Guernsey artists to do in his very best style three views for me, a centre and two side ones, somewhere about 15 or 18 inches long with a due corresponding breadth, either in oils, water-colours or body-colours. The centre I should like to be a view of the town from Castle Cornet, and the other two views of interest in the island, either of your or the artist's own selection. Even if in oils, they ought to be glazed with neat frames, on which there should be but little gilding & few gold/gilt ornaments. I suppose £20 would pay for the set. These I should be very, very glad of for my sitting room.

Tell William that if he likes to keep *Henley on Thames*, he may do so. If he won't accept it as a present, let him send me something to adorn my room instead.

I wish I knew what you would like from this. My gun has long been idle, & I suppose you've had enough of Himalayan birds. I hope to be able to visit Dehli next vacation, where I may pick up something worth the boys' acceptance ...

LETTER LXXV

From MAUGER MONK, Mullingar House, Landour
To ISABELLA MONK.

5 JUNE 1848

My Dear Isabella,

Your long letter of the 17th April arrived yesterday evening just as I returned from Church, and though the latest safe date for the transmission of letters by the mail of the 19th from Bombay was announced for yesterday; yet I venture on a few lines to say how thankful I am to you for your kindness in thinking of my wants & wishes in the matter of the drawings, about wh, however, I regret that I should have put you to expence. It won't, however, be money badly laid out for me; for I shall visit Dehli next vacation, & though everything that comes from Europe possesses an infinite value in my eyes, yet I dare say the curiosities & bijouteries of the East, coming from me, will not be without their value to you. The coats, which were sent to me in 1841 are almost as good as when they arrived. The nethers are worn out, but they lasted for years. I mention this to shew you how careful I am of all that comes from home, that home I may possibly never see again, and if I do, sadly changed from what I left it. You shall have a monthly sketch either in pencil or pen & ink. In the first I have been pronounced, by Coll Everest, the late Surveyor Genl of India, to be the best and most correct draughtsman in the country, and he was a competent judge. I enclose a short note for Magrath, which perhaps you will not object to forward. I wrote to him on business yesterday and as I cannot pre-pay my letters, owing to this mail going via Marseilles, I am not disposed to put him to more expence than that of the rather heavy epistle sent yesterday. The rains have set in with fearful violence, my garden-walls washed down, & other injuries done to the place to the tune of some Rs 500, but these are losses wh we yearly look for, being one of the penalties we must pay for the advantage of a healthy, bracing mountain-climate. My darling boy repays the kisses four-fold. He is, thank heaven, a healthy, lively tho' very little fellow with such a curly pate of beautiful but short brown hair, finer than silk.

In some of your next mention the result of poor John Harvey's mésaventure. I've taken a great interest in the unfortunate fellow's mishap, for I cannot believe him guilty.

Will you believe it? I'm trying to teach myself the flageolet, for of an evening I do not like to strain my eyes too long over drawing, writing or reading, as they are not without lots of occupation from sun-rise till some hours after sun-down, and I imagine a little music wd make me less gloomy than I am sometimes disposed to be.

This, though short, will probably be the quickest reply you ever recd from this part of the world, to wh I have, ever since the news of the last French Revolution arrived, been pondering how I could with advantage to yourselves bring over both you & Madge, as to the safest asylum I know in the present agitated state of Europe, which is, I fear, likely to be still more convulsed than it is.

When you write to Aunt Wm give her my most affectionate love and say I will write to her shortly. The love & kisses you may also give to dear Uncle Joe & Aunt Eliza, but continue to make my letters do for you all, for I am inundated with daily correspondence, which must be answered, & in the intervals between school my pen knows no rest. Remember me kindly to all inquiring friends, amongst whom you may perhaps be able to find some fine girl, of a serious turn & possessing a few accomplishments willing to take a mountaineer-brother for better or WUSS. Love & kisses to Madge. Tell her I'm "kuffa" (angry) that she won't write ...

P.S. Don't forget the Act of Parliament.

Mussoorie, once the Queen of Hills, no longer fits the image of a quaint hill-station, where even old landmarks like the Clock Tower have vanished

LETTER LXXVI

More about the insurance policy.

17 & 18 JULY 1848

From Freeth, Agent, To M. F. Monk:

The Bank Directors at Meerut have agreed to renewal of credit.

18 AUGUST 1848

From NICHOLAS MAGRATH, Guernsey

To MAUGER MONK, [Landour].

12 OCTOBER 1848

My Dear Mauger,

In accordance with your last letter I forward herewith, your father's watch chain & seal, which I trust will reach you safely, your books are really not worth sending to you. Your sisters have had the list of them but I presume they were too lazy to forward them or copy them for you. However they are at ... [damaged] ... firm directions how they are to be disposed of. I believe William sold his share for a few pounds. As to your French stock I gave Lemasurier your directions (indeed your letter) so that I presume the stock is in your name your child & mine as trustee but as I have not seen the inscription I cannot tell you exactly the wording—I would therefore in order to save you expence, recommend your sending me a power of attorney to act for you, & also write to LeMasurier to give up all papers he may have of yours (as your procureur for the estate of your father) otherwise you must correspond with him as he can only give you information on these points. Old Uncle Joe is still alive & no bringing him to book although I try all I can to do so. William has been away these last two months in France & has returned looking very well, so that we may now be able to work out a division of your Mothers property which ought to have taken place 34 years ago.

In your next letter just tell me in paucis verbis what you mean, what you wish, & precisely how I am to act, & let me hear no such nonsense as not being aware of what you have written or what has transpired. As this is a species of humbug I do not understand, ergo, if you intend that I shall act for you, you must be plain, commonly sensible & fully recollect all that transpires. We are all thank God well. Henry is I dare say by this time at ascension on his way to the Coast of Africa, having commenced his carreer [sic] about two months back, the others I fear will take the same bent, however I am determined they shall have it as far as I am concerned. Let me hear succinctly & distinctly from you & when I understand you I shall feel pleasure in being of use to you then,

Your affectionate brother-in-law
N. Magrath.

LETTER LXXVII

From SARAH MAGRATH. Ditto.

13 OCTOBER 1848

My Dear Mauger,

My little folks now take up so much of my time that, I am become a worse correspondent than ever; Henry sailed from Plymouth in the "Pantaloon" brig on the first of August and we are now in daily expectation of hearing from him from Ascension or St. Helena. He wrote from Madeira, had got over sea sickness & ... [damaged] ... life comfortably[?]. Miles has I think made up his mind to be a medical man and is going on very steadily at college he is in the 5th form and would have been put into the 6th at midsummer but I do not much fancy the Principal, Mr. Corfe the Vice Principal being à mon gout a much more efficient master. Jack & Charley are both in the lower school and Ellen growing a sturdy healthy girl. How does your dear boy get on, does the climate affect his health. Let me know all about yourself and him when you write, as we hold no communication whatever with Isabella or Margaret. Nor indeed does it ever appear likely, we shall do so again therefore it is useless to transmit any messages either through or for them. The French dividends have been again paid last month but matters are far from being settled there. Wm who is just returned from Paris where he has been for the last two months says that there is a feeling that some new revolution may daily be expected but from which quarter it may be looked for is a problem which the wisest heads will not venture to solve. Still the opinion is that whichever of the five parties into which France is now divided hold the reins of government that the public debt will be respected. I would gladly send you the *Illustrated News* had I not promised it to my boy to whom we have an opportunity of sending them on the lst of every month as a man of war leaves either Plymouth or Portsmo' with a mail for the squadron on the African station regularly. The dear boy looked very well in his midshipman's uniform. He is very like what you were at his age except the colour of his eyes. Cousin Lambe's second boy John is also in the Navy in the "Asia" in S. America, his eldest son Hugh is here dying of consumption, an amiable youth of 19[17?]. The brother whom he calls "his bitter pill" from whom he has been separated legally for some years is here also and the two girls but it is really pitiable to witness the effect of the parents ill temper, the only fault alleged on either side in the neglect both mental & physical of the poor children. Lambe himself lives at Bath. Mr. Little has just buried his second wife who I understand was no loss. Chas Whiteford (& the Smiths) with whom we hold no intercourse has six boys; but really I have met with so much unkindness & want of good faith from all belonging to me that beyond my own children & husband I am almost tempted to look for none. Still if I can be of use either to you or your dear child (who has no mother) I may perhaps be more really kind than those whose promises are much fairer. God bless you & ...

LETTER LXXVIII

From M. F. Monk, Landour
To Major Freeth, Agent, Mussoorie.
Monk sends in policy No.859 with premiums paid to 15 Feb. 1849.

16 OCTOBER 1848

From MAUGER MONK, Mullingar House, Landour
To NICHOLAS MAGRATH, Guernsey.

18 OCTOBER 1848

My Dear Magrath,

Ever since the receipt of your letter in May I have been looking anxiously for the papers you promised to send me, as well as, of late, an answer to mine of the 4th June, [141 above] but I fear I have somehow or other unwittingly given offence, as in that letter I asked you to continue sending me the *Illustrated London News* wh, supposing you may not have had time to write, might have been sent as a symptom that friendly relations were about to be restored. I have not heard of the loss of any of the mails this year, so I presume my letter came duly to hand. I hope it did as it contained my thanks for all you have done, & full authority for you to invest my dividends (French) in the same way you did your own. It contained many other matters, some of wh I recollect, sed nunc enumerare longum erit [?] & others I completely forget; but I do not remember that there was anything in it, wh could annoy or offend either you or Sarah. It has of course occurred to me, that in the preparations for & subsequent departure of your eldest boy on his first voyage, you must not only have been busily engaged, but have had scarce time to turn yr thoughts to the Himalayas lest then you may forget me altogether, & even neglect to drink my health & success on Xmas-day, I now write to tell you that I am within the land of the living, anxious to hear from you, from Sarah, from anyone, indeed, who will condescend to give the poor mountain-pedagogue an occasional line, driving a very good business, & expecting it to be more than doubled next season, as my old employer, MacKinnon, gives up school next month to turn brewer & army-accoutrement maker in succession to his father in law, old Bohlé, "who retires", as the Army-List saith. My new school-house will accommodate three-score or more boarders.

The express to the 7th Septr has just arrived, but the letters cannot reach till the day after to-morrow, or I should delay this in hopes of having a communication from you to reply to. I hear that Harry's first cruise is to the Coast of Africa. If true, I could have wished him a more agreeable station, and pleasanter duties than chasing slavers & boat service in the Gambia & Senegal. Is not his skipper my old friend, Sydney Grenfell, with whom I once took a cruise, pedestrian, experimental & exploratory, from Plymo almost to the Land's End. Don't make a bad pun on it, & say the S[c]illy Isles must have been our destination.

It's an ill-wind that blows nobody good. MacKinnon's giving up is a wind-fall, & so in a manner is the new Panjaub War, as scholars who wod otherwise have gone home, remain this winter with us—pas being on service. The only unpleasant drawbacks to this are—before they march pas can't pay outstandings, they never remit during a campaign, & no one ever received a farthing, should they be knocked on the head, that sink of Calcutta iniquity, the Registrar's Office in the Supreme Court absorbing like a whirlpool whatever trifle their estates may produce. Bengal Military officers nearly all die bankrupt.

I received a verbal intimation the other day thro' Lieutt McAuliffe who stayed two months with me, from Genl Whish, that he had some communication from home to make to me. Did you send any by him? For the old gentn is now entrenched for two or three months, having been obliged to raise the siege of Mooltan & wait till reinforcements join him; so that it is not very likely that he & I will soon meet.

Could not William give me a few lines before he started for Paris, or am I on his black list? Can you tell? With all love to Sarah & the children. I remain, my dear Magrath,

Your's affectionately,
M. Fitzh Monk.

LETTER LXXIX

"No.1322" by M. Fitzh. Monk.

28 OCTOBER 1848

"Know all men ... I, M.F.M. of Landour ... schoolmaster ..." He mortgages his "estate at Landour called Mullingar" for 8,000 Rs to N.W. Bank of India, with Insurance Policy for 10,000 Rs as collateral. Witnessed by I. R. Lewin & ... Eaton.

CRASH, FLIGHT AND DEATH 1849

LETTER LXXIX

From MAUGER MONK, Mullingar, Landour
To NICHOLAS MAGRATH, Manor House, Guernsey.
Endorsed: Guernsey 7 Ju 1849.

21 APRIL 1849

My Dear Magrath,

I hope that you have received my letters of the 2nd and 25th Feby and that Mallet & Co paid my dividends in London, so that my bill upon Drummond was met some time during the present month. My best thanks to you for what you have done and the trouble you have had in money matters, but I want you to do another thing for me, which I asked you to do once before, but which, owing to the unsettled state of the times, you said could not then be managed, namely to raise me the loan of a thousand pounds on the security of my scrip, now, I trust, out of Mr. Le Masurier's and in your hands, the dividends to be received by the lender for eleven years, which, as the annexed memo: shows, will pay capital and interest at 5 per cent. I find paying the bank here 12 per cent a heavy incubus on my exertions & rather than take money from it, I have suspended the completion of the wing of my school, so that it looks like a donkey with one ear, & we are obliged to make shift without much of the accommodation absolutely necessary in a school. I could very well keep down the interest and pay it half-yearly in London, but I suspect the Guernsey folks regard Indian remittances as things that may be, and so have put my offer in the above form. I could get a tenant if I wished to give up here, and a good one too, but without sound security I shall not do so and then, independent of the dividends, come home on £200 per annum. While health & strength remain, I shall stick to the school though I often long to visit Guernsey, unless, indeed, as I have had a hint government wish to have the estate. Govt here is always a liberal purchaser, & should it take up my place, I should get a handsome sum for it. Now, like a good fellow, kindly see & transact this matter for me.

India is now again as quiet as ever, the Punjaub annexed, & the commisioners hard at work settling the country, which will doubly repay Honble John most handsomely. It has been bought at a heavy sacrifice of life through old Gough's incapacity & want of temper, but the battle of Goojerat in a measure redeemed Chillianwala, though the old fool made no attempt to exterminate the Sikhs, as he might have done. What is William doing? [He had died on the 21st March.] Surely he might write to a poor div whose daily labour commences at dawn & ends at bed-time. Give my love to him and tell him how welcome a yarn will be bimonthly, if he won't write oftener. So poor Uncle Joe, the last of my mother's brothers, is gone at last after many years of sickness & suffering. With him I presume has gone all chance of realising what was our mother's property, whatever that may have been, for I have not the remotest idea & have hitherto vainly sought to be informed. What accounts does the young reefer give of himself? I hope satisfactory. My love to him when you write, & with love & kisses to the rest of the flock & Sarah, I remain, my dear Magrath,

Your's affectionately,
M. Fitzh Monk.

[Memo of details of repayment of proposed loan attached.]

LETTER LXXX

From MAUGER MONK, Mullingar, Landour
To NICHOLAS MAGRATH, [Guernsey.] Black-edged.

14 JUNE 1849

My Dear Magrath,

I awaited the arrival of the 2nd day's batch of letters from Bombay, the mail from England to May 7th being in, to see if there would be ought for me. As yet I have not received any letter, & can delay no longer to thank you for yours of the 15th April, [157 above] which has placed my unfortunate brother's death in a light I had scarcely, from the short account given of it in the "Atlas for India" & said to be an extract from the star, been able to entertain a hope of. Poor fellow! His fate has, indeed, been a warning, a very painful lesson wh I probably needed more. In former days than I do now, for it is a long time since my lips have been acquainted with spirit, or a third glass of wine has entered them on the same day. Isabella wrote by a previous mail to that which brought your letter, but gave no particulars. Truly do I hope that Sarah has recovered the blow it appears to have been to her.

I regret that for want of proper explanation I shod have drawn on myself a lecture for my draft for the £120, a sum I should not so summarily have drawn, had I not been disappointed for the dozenth time in the receipt of a sum of Rs 2000, due to me these three or four years by a Major Nash of the Native Cavalry. In this instance I did not look for a disappointment as his commission was at stake for "conduct unbecoming the character" &c, the man having solemnly pledged himself in writing to the Commr-in-Chief to liquidate my claim on the arrival of the mail, either in July or August, 1848. The scoundrel took advantage of the C-in-C: being in the field, the subsequent change of chiefs, and has not to this hour paid me one farthing. I have four other "honourable" men on my books for nearly similar amounts, & many for smaller. Their conduct or rather, civility, has alone prevented them from being handed up to their "betters".

I know nothing more likely to ensure my not drawing again on Drummonds than a compliance with the request, made in my letter of the 21st April [159 above] and which I wod again urge as likely to be of the most essential service to me; a request, the carrying out of which your lawyer wod, I am sure, with such ample security, readily undertake. The increase by the dividends from poor William's estate, would materially shorten the time, in wh the sum of £1000 with intt at 5 per cent would be repaid to the lender, and the income would become available at a time when I shod require it for Hugh's education at home; and what is of some consideration to me, I should not feel those expenses to be a drag upon me, the source, from wh they would be paid, being one I had not availed myself of. I would add too, the possibility of a second family, and the very easy reply I could make to little Hugh's step-mother (should he ever have one,) at my giving an expensive education to my first-born, when it might not be in my power to give her children the advantages of one in Europe also. If you manage this matter for me, and I feel sure you will, let the holder of the scrip give a receipt in duplicate for it, one copy to be transmitted to me & receive his first instalment from March's (1850) dividends. September's would be mine, of course.

I do not think I shod be acting justly to any after-arrival were I to transfer my quota of poor Wm's scrip to that now standing in your name, conjointly with mine & Hugh's, so let it go, please, to mine simply. Au reste, as I am desirous to become a holder of Company's stock & be prepared for finally settling in this country, sell & turn into money anything else that may be coming to me; books, silver, share of the house, & when realisable, my quota of my mother's estate. Of the last your explanation only confuses me more & more, as I have not the remotest idea of the nature, value or anything else connected with Guernsey quarters, tho' a boyish recollection of advertisements anent "quartiers de rente" & "quartiers de froment" in the Gazette still remains. Margaret, I am told, values the house at Ann's Place in £1000, of wh 2/5ths would be somewhere about £400. A beautiful little property, adjoining mine, wh rents for £80 per annum or rather Rs 800, is for sale, and I would sooner possess that to add to my income here than property in Europe to add to the dividends there. If my fifths then suit either yourself or Sarah at the above, take them, if not, let Isabella or Margaret have them. The owner of the place I mention is so anxious to return this winter to Scotland, that I see every chance of getting a desirable addition to my estate for Rs 3600 or Rs 3700. Of silver I have good store, and if William's was valuable, it wd be a pity to separate it. His signet-ring I shd prize, if you wod part with it & as those things are not made in the Himalaya, get me before you send it, some 800 or 1000 wafers of various hues, black inclusive, from the die.

My objects then are briefly these: To make the French dividends a provision for my boy; & to realise all else in cash to provide as I may deem best, for an addition to my income now, in this country, securing thus a competence both for old age, or a second family. The school goes on very well. We have about 60 pupils, inclusive of 38 boarders in spite of the opposition of the Mussoorie chaplain, who has an exclusive establishment, to wh the sons of officers, civ or mil only are admitted. The measles broke out amongst us yesterday, I regret to say. We anticipate a formidable opposition next season, as a clergyman of the Ch of Engld, backed by two able assistants, takes the field against us, and is expected to arrive in September. My boy continues to thrive and is very healthy. Of late too he has shot up a good deal. The existence of aunts & uncle in Europe he cannot yet perfectly comprehend. His aunt, uncle & grandfather here are very, very fond of him, and the first is a complete mother to him, washing, clothing & taking care of him herself, & having his little bed in her room.

I trust your accounts from the pantaloon are still everything that you and Sarah can desire, and that some, one, at all events, of the other three have made up their minds to try their fortunes on some other element than the unstable ocean.

Give my best love & kisses to them all, and dear little Nelly, in particular, & believe me to be

Your's affectionately,
M. Fitzh Monk.

N.D. [Likely to be mid-1849]

"Debts in India"—an unsigned paper. To bank 12,000 & Mr. Jones 1,300 = 13,300 Rs. Plus 1,280 to various named creditors, and interest of 156 to Mr. Jones and 720 interest to bank.

Total: Rs 15,456. "Mem: There is a large amount due to Ford & Co., 656 S, but this I can realise, I hope, from the estate of my wife's relatives." "Property in Europe: 2/5 of Wm.'s house: £400, & share of his plate £20. Of my mother's property I can get no account further than that it is in court nor of the balance which may be in my favour in the banker's hands. Invested property: francs. In the French 5 per cent from my father's est: 3,000, from my brother's 500 = 3,500."

[Mauger Monk married again on 9 August 1849.]

LETTER LXXXI

Receipt of Rs.250 by N. W. Bank of India (Mussoorie Branch) from M. F. Monk: life insurance premium.

28 AUGUST 1849

From MAUGER MONK, Landour
To NICHOLAS MAGRATH, [Guernsey].

6 NOVEMBER 1849

My Dear Magrath,

I purpose leaving this on my return to Europe early next month, going first thro' Meerut to the Ganges, down wh I sail, & home then from Calcutta by ship. Illness for the last two months caused by enlargement & torpidity of liver have in the doctor's opinion rendered a voyage necessary, so instead of merely taking a jaunt to the Sandheads, I journey homewards altogether, purposing to settle in any nice sea-port town, where I am not known, & where I can obtain some not too heavy employment. The non-sale of the house has sadly disappointed me, & I am in consequence indebted to a friend for the means of leaving this part of the world. On the lst Decr I give him bills on London for £250, at 3 months' date, to enable Isabella to lodge that amount with Drummond. I have written to her by to-day's dâk, & requested her, should she be unable or unwilling to advance me the amount, to signify the same to you, that you may sell out the French rentes left me by poor William, which, in the event of my sister's non-compliance I authorise you to do. I have told her that my 2/5ths of the house are her security. It wod be rather a rough greeting to be hugged by a bum-bailiff on landing in London especially as I bring a wife, with me. I was not to have been married till the spring of 1850, but the lady, who had adopted my wife when an orphan, having become insane—the suite of a puerperal fever, & her husband's affairs having got into a mess, in wh I am somewhat involved, & he obliged to go to Calcutta, the marriage was hurried on at a time the wee body who is only sixteen ought to have been going to school as originally intended. However she is good-hearted, good-tempered, & industrious.

My illness has been a very severe one, and the worst part was the frightful depression of spirits, with wh it was accompanied. The wee wife was a great comfort to me during the whole time.

His aunt having on Hugh's account refused several good offers, I have consented to leave him with them till I have a settled habitation: they tried hard to have him left with them till he was twelve years of age, but to this I wod not consent. They, however, firmly believe I shall be back in the mountains before two years are over my head. The employment I shod like would be an Insurance Office Agency, wh might give me from £90 to £120 per annum for hard work I do not find myself fitted, tho' the doctor assures me that, notwithstanding the affection of my liver must be of some standing, (I can't believe it) I shall be all right again after the first good sea-sickness, a complaint I never yet knew. But enough—love to Sarah & love & kisses to little Ellen, & the boys at home, & Harry, when you write. What was the matter in the pantaloon, all the screws appear to have been loose according to the papers? I can't be at home much before June, & will be ready for work in July, if I can get a berth: Southampton, Portsmo or Brighton would suit me.

Your's, affectionately,
M. Fitzh Monk.

LETTER LXXXII

From MAUGER MONK, Landour
To NICHOLAS MAGRATH, [Guernsey].
[Mauger died at Meerut on 9 December 1849.]

21 NOVEMBER 1849

My Dear Magrath,

Recd yours of the 4th Octr, [163 above] & am much obliged for the particulars contained. The amount will be useful as I leave on the 3rd Decr for Calcutta, and thence to the Cape, instead of coming direct to Europe as I at first intended, & mentioned to you in my letter of 7th inst, wh, having gone via Calcutta, will probably not come to hand many, if any, days before this. As I shall be a stranger in the land of the Hottentots, kindly let me have a copy of my account with Drummond to meet me "care of Postmaster, Cape Town, S.Africa" with a negotiable letter of credit for balance, for I shall be at fault, should Sir Harry Smith, to whom I wrote four days ago, not be able to give me a berth. I do not expect to reach the bay before the early part of April, so kindly let there be a few lines to meet me. As to my dividends I do not know the exact sum to draw for. On the 13th Oct I drew in favour of a Mr. J.G. Jones for £70, believing the plate-money would have been paid in. In general I have only drawn for £60, though I think that a trifle less than the half yearly dividends amounted to. In future, I am aware they will be something more. Hence my anxiety to have a statement of the bankers' account; in short to know to a fraction how I shall stand with them when the items specified in your letter, inclusive of the dividends for March, shall have been paid in. In altering the plan of my movements, I have also shortened the advance made me by a friend by £100, & have only borrowed from him £150 instead of £250, as mentioned in my letter of the 7th. I have, on the faith of my two sisters' expressed willingness I have the letter by me now to place £400 for my two-fifths of the house at my disposal, asked them to assist me with the latter amount (£250). This must now be altered, for I suspect their purse-strings to be tight ones, and as my bills for £150, drawn in favour of Mr. Herbert Grant Scott will become due on the 15th March, kindly send word to Drummond to meet them at that date. The seven or eight days interest I will most willingly pay rather than have the bills returned. The Scott family have been kind friends to me, & I shod regret any thing going amiss as regards them. I drew at 4 mths date on the 15th Novr for £150. I have carefully looked over the different powers sent by Le Mesurier, but find only those for sale of stock & transfer. The one I sent you I drew up myself, for no form ever came. You will, inter alia, have to send me one to the Cape. My school, I am sorry to say, will not now afford more than a respectable maintenance for one master. The clergy have it all their own way. Two have started, & a third is expected to land daily. In another year no schoolmaster, who cannot clap "Revd" before, & A.B. or A.M. after his name can stand. My brother-in-law takes my estate as, I may say, an adventure, for he has nothing, & will keep dear little Hugh till I am settled. He is too young to travel yet, for, altho' five years old, he is but a "wee" fellow, wiry, good-looking, healthy and active.

The account you give of your own little household makes me almost wish to be the "father of a family". I hope to see them all flourishing like young bay-trees, should the fates be unpropitious at the Cape, wh something strikes me they will not be. As to continuing the life of a pedagogue, I can't. Bilious, & disgusted with tardy payments, in many instances no payments at all, I am about to leave teaching to the padres, for it is useless trying to compete with them. Of the nonpayments I give you but one example in an officer of the Arty, Captn Daniell, who died in Ferozepore, owing me not only 1600 Rs for his children's schoolg but 560 Rs, money lent him to join the army before Mooltan, when he had but 10 Rs in the world & not a tent to cover him. His liabilities at his decease proved to be upwards of 31,000 Rs—his assets 937 Rs, of which 1400 Rs were due as a retrenchment to Govt.

If I meet with no luck at the Cape, I'll be home as soon as possible, & there I may meet with some employment, tho' I know the market to be overstocked.

Love & kisses to Sarah & the bairns, not forgetting the young Cyclops, who I hope to see some day with his lst swab, & believe me, with all sort of soft sayings from my silent spouse,

Your's, affectionately.
M. Fitzh Monk.

P.S. What is the nor of the scrip left me by Wm. I wish to specify it in my will.

LETTER LXXXIII

From The Reverend ISAAC LEWIN, Landour Academy.
To (implicitly) NICHOLAS MAGRATH.
Black-edged.

27 DECEMBER 1849

Dear Sir,

Upon me devolves the melancholy task of conveying intelligence which you can by no means be prepared to hear the place from which this is addressed, and the person whom you know to have been connected with it will arouse you worst apprehensions; these it is my painful duty to confirm by announcing the sudden death of poor Monk.

You are aware of his intention of leaving India for England. His arrangements were completed and he left Landour on the morning of the 5th Inst in the best of health. On his way down I find he exposed himself to the cold and immediately upon his arrival was attacked by Croup. Medical advice was taken, and as far as I can learn by the enquiries I made in Meerut, he was treated for this desease[sic], tho' from the certificate of death wh I obtained from Dr. Spencer who attended upon him I find his death was occasioned by the "bursting of an aneurism". These are the only particulars I can gather concerning poor Monk's death. He died on the morning of the 9th and was interred by a few acquaintance in Meerut. I have just returned from Meerut, where I went on hearing of the above sad intelligence, and, in order to save this mail, can write but a few hasty lines. By next mail I will have been better informed upon the subject and will write to you more fully.

If a stranger's sympathy would be accepted, I would willingly offer mine. My intimacy with the deceased has made me acquainted with many domestic matters in England, and I cannot express the sorrow I feel at the late calamities which have befallen your family of late. To expect consolation from another source than that from which all draw & are satisfied would be vain, & to him—the Consolation of Israel—wd point. It is so hard in such a moment to say "God, thy Will be done". Yet if we have faith we must; and altho' He moves in a mysterious may his wonders to perform, He in the end shows all has been for our good.

In a letter such as the present it is painful to write upon business. The subject is however of much importance and I must ask you whether Monk sent home his will to you. It is nowhere amongst his effects here. On this as on other matters I will write fully by next mail—every moment lessens my chance of sending this by the present.

The enclosed makes the same announcement but as I do not know Miss Monk's address, I must trouble you to forward it. Believe me,

Yours faithfully,
I. R. Lewin.

1850 AND BEYOND. ALL IS EXPLAINED?

LETTER LXXXIV

From The Revd ISAAC LEWIN, Landour Academy
To (implicitly) NICHOLAS MAGRATH.

5 FEBRUARY 1850

Dear Sir,

Owing to my being for the winter in a very retired place with my school, I have unconsciously allowed one mail to pass by, without giving you the promised details. The sad event announced in my last, was so very sudden that tho' I have received many letters on the subject I can add but little to what I have already written and that little very unimportant. The determination to go home was very suddenly formed by poor Monk and on the receipt of certain, letters from Guernsey which prevented his concluding certain arrangements satisfactorily. On the morning of the 5th Decr 1849 he left this on his way to Meerut, intending to float down the River Ganges in a boat from Ghurmoshtesur, a place about 30 miles from Meerut. The first stage from this was Saharunpore where he arrived during the afternoon of the 5th and at nightfal started again by a mode of conveyance called "the truck". (This is a rude cab with sufficient accommodation for two, and a seat outside for the driver). Unfortunately he left the covered part of the conveyance and took a seat by the side of the driver, and as a consequence caught a severe cold before he arrived at Meerut. I must here mention the nights during the winter here are excessively chill and the dews very heavy. The cold was not neglected on his arrival, but he did not take the necessary care of himself after a journey, for the day was spent in visiting some friends here, and he very imprudently attended lodge where he kept up until one or two the next morning. On the morning of the 7th his voice had sunk almost to a whisper and he experienced a feeling of suffocation. He now consulted Dr. Spencer, Surgeon of Artillery, and considered a very skillful person, who bled him very copiously administered some medicine, and I believe leeches were applied afterwards. The treatment relieved him for a time but during the afternoon of the 8th he was worse and from the most particular enquiries I have made it would appear he apprehended danger. The owner of the house in which he lodged was attracted to his room about midnight by some noise and on entearing [sic] found him walking backwards and forwards very rapidly. On seeing this person enter he made a sign for him to strike him between his shoulders, at the same time signifying he was, being suffocated; this was done, and being partially relieved was laid on his bed where he, two hours after, that is, 2 o'clock on the morning of the 9th, expired without uttering a word, and without a struggle. I have unwillingly and at the expense of inviting[?] many melancholy thoughts dwelt so minutely on the subject; as I would rather have it said that I was too minute than that I had not written satisfactorily.

From all I can learn, he died fully prepared to appear before his maker. Altho' when at Landour somewhat careless of the one all important subject, yet during the last few days of his life he appeared fully impressed with this subject, and his stern silence during the last day and a half and deep meditation which he did not even allow his wife to interrupt, plainly showed he was preparing his mind for the great and awful change. It may be, that God in his infinite and unsearchable wisdom took him to himself in the very moment when he found him repentant.

His son, Hugh, he had left with me; not intending to have sent for him for years, if indeed at all. Altho' most intimate with him for the last eight years and well acquainted with the principal transactions of his private life, the short and natural withdrawal of confidence on account of his second marriage does not allow me to write with any confidence on this subject, but from the brief outline he gave of the subjects of his last letters home, I fear his real motives for going home were not given nor his actual intentions touched upon. That he had once before thought of going home I am aware, but this idea was altogether given up before he contracted his second marriage; indeed he told me three or four times before he left that had he thought (seriously) of going home he would not have married.

I expect a reply to my first letter next month, upon the receipt of which I'll give as clear a statement of his affairs as I can. In this matter I trust you will forgive me if I ask you to divest yourself of the feelings of a stranger towards me and enable us to act cordially in this one matter, the care and guardianship of our nephew. I remain, dear sir,

Yours very faithfully,
I.R. Lewin.

P.S. I have not written by this mail to Miss Monk; and if you could kindly send this for their perusal you would not oblige me but them, as my letter to them contained a very few lines barely announcing the decease of their brother.

LETTER LXXXV

From Drummonds, London to Nicholas Magrath, Guernsey.
A bill for £150 on the late M. F. Monk has been presented,
but his account only holds £1-17-1.

22 FEBRUARY 1850

Ditto: £21. Note by N. Magrath giving £200
to Le Mesurier to cover it.

25 FEBRUARY 1850

From Drummonds to N. Magrath acknowledging
his statement that he would be responsible for
the late M. F. Monk's account.

8 MAY 1850

From The Revd ISAAC LEWIN, Landour Academy
To (implicitly) NICHOLAS MAGRATH.

30 JULY 1850

My Dear Sir,

I have been prevented from writing to you by long and continued indisposition. Tho' regretting this delay greatly, I could not possibly avoid it.

As I have before informed you, Monk died in Meerutt, on his way to England, and when leaving Landour had, of course, settled his Indian affairs. The property he had with him in Meerutt, and which his widow took possession of, was all he had in India, at the time of his death.

It will not take many words to give an account of Monk's property that which he at any time had here. The Rajpore estate was bought by him for a much larger amount than it was worth, and not being able to pay this amount, the estate was given up, and two thousand rupees paid to the seller, in lieu of payment in full. This was effected in 1847. After this he bought property in Landour for eight thousand rupees, and subsequently added to it, at a cost of between four and five thousand rupees. When arrangements were being made for leaving India, this property, at cost price valuation, was, in proper form, made over to me for taking upon myself the payment of Monk's debt amounting to seventeen thousand and odd rupees—he promising to liquidate the balance from England.

During many months before his marriage Monk's habits had become very irregular, and his companions such as he would not have approved of himself in moments of reflection, as friends, tho' they had been acquaintances for a length of time. He married to break himself of these habits, and to settle for good in India. The choice was not such as his best friends would have approved of, for the girl was of no family or education, and considerably younger.

You will now be prepared to hear that the reasons alleged by Monk, were not the real ones for leaving India. He certainly had on several occasions spoken of leaving, but every thought (if it ever was seriously entertained) was abandoned when he determined upon marrying a second time. It was subsequent to this, when he suddenly found his liabillities [sic] press too heavily, and he was persuaded he could obtain no assistance from home, that he resolved upon leaving India. Since his marriage I had purposely withdrawn myself from him, and tho' still intimate, I had not his former confidence. I did not therefore hear of this resolution, until it was too late, to make proper arrangements. I am of opinion that if timely attention had been paid, matters might have been so adjusted as to prevent the unfortunate circumstances which afterwards occurred. His plan, that which he had decided upon finally was communicated to me. This was to leave India without the knowledge of his creditors, and let them seize upon his property and make the most of it. I could not approve of a plan which I looked upon as dishonourable and unworthy, not only of the character and position he had held in society [sic], but of the honourable feelings which had, so far as my knowledge of him extended, at all times guided him. Had I had money sufficient, no difficulty could have arisen for I would have most cheerfully given up all for his benefit. The influence or names I could have commanded were lost by some circumstances attending my recent marriage. Under these circumstances I recommended the course which he ultimately adopted, and which I have mentioned in the beginning of my letter.

Hugh, Monk's only child, was left under my guardianship, with every thing to make my office and authority complete. Since the death of his mother, my sister, I have had his exclusive charge. This guardianship I should wish to retain and I have been advised I have a right to it. I have no wish to separate him from his other relations. I took charge of him in his infancy and this charge which commenced then I am desirous of holding until he can take care of himself. His father's and my views of education were so similar, and we have so frequently conversed upon this subject, that I cannot err in following out his father's wishes. I shall be glad to receive, at all times, suggestions from you, and his friends. Indeed, I should very miserably discharge my duties of a guardian were I to disregard any advice likely to benefit him.

After his death a life policy of the value of 12000 Rs (twelve thousand rupees) became due. It is as yet unadjusted, and I fear its adjusting will become tedious as it is hampered by conditions wh I have not yet learned. The last instalment of premium was overdue, and as soon as this came to my knowledge it was paid as tho' from Monk. I believe it was not too late. As soon as I get over my heavy arrears of correspondence I will look into the matter.

With regard to your letter and the facts mentioned in it. I doubt the validity of the will executed in 1837 at Chatham. Subsequent marriages and the birth of children have revoked it. Monk then died intestate, and his widow possesses the power of administering. This right can be of little consequence if the nature of the property be considered. That portion in Europe is, with an unimportant exception, invested in the French funds, and the beneficial interest seems to be exclusively in the son of the deceased. The legal interest, however, seems to be in yourself and Hugh jointly, so that the whole of the property must stand until Hugh is of age. The bulk then is disposed of. The portion in India is easily settled, if no unnecessary obstacle be thrown in the way. The widow is not likely to object, as she is very inclined to marry, and with a pretty face and a few thousands must succeed.

I would now ask what you intend doing. I have papers left with me by Monk which give me an account of his Europe property, but I should wish to have your opinion on the subject.

Among the many debts I took upon myself is one of £130. It is a note drawn by Monk and accepted by me; this becomes due on the 3rd Oct next and my means being exhausted in paying the more pressing ones, I do not know how to meet this but by borrowing. I can claim a balance, as you will have seen, from the estate, but it is not my intention to throw any difficulties in the settlement of affairs. This amount might be given to me from the balance in London belonging to Monk. As the note is drawn by him I do not know how I can be denied the amount. When released, I shall send it to you to hold, to save you from any anticipated unpleasantness. In this matter pray do not keep me in suspense. The heavy liabilities I have incurred on account of the deceased being thrown among men of business I shall find it perhaps impossible to raise the amount, and the consequence will be unpleasant.

It will be needless to speak of myself. I have had occasion to mention my name too frequently already. Money is the test of friendship in these days and if the test be allowed, I have acted as a friend—others may pronounce me injudicious, but it has been to the best of my ability. To the same I must point as a proof of my honesty of purpose. Under the load I have taken upon myself, it is very probable I shall sink. It is here I have property, but it is dead stock and unproductive; to-day worth so much, next year not one-third of its value. The utmost it can do is to save me from dishonour. If matters take this issue I must begin life anew. A dreary prospect for one who has lately married and expects a large family.

Yours sincerely,
I. R. Lewin.

P.S. I find I cannot get the certificates to-day, you may depend upon receiving them by next mail. You will, hereafter, under any circumstances hear from me by return of mail.

LETTER LXXXVI

Statement of Account: Mauger F. Monk Esq.
with Messrs. Drummond.

1847-1850

Power of Attorney from ANNE MONK, widow,
to ISAAC REDGROVE LEWIN to authorize him
to collect all moneys etc. due to her.

21 DECEMBER 1850

[Text incorrectly dated 1850]
From the Revd ISAAC LEWIN, Landour Academy
To NICHOLAS MAGRATH, Guernsey.

6 JANUARY 1851

My Dear Sir,

Your letter of the 15th Oct arrived later than it ought to have, but I hasten to reply in the hope of being in time for the mail which will leave Bombay on the 17th Instant.

I thought I had made my letter sufficiently explicit on all points, and in giving a statement of Monk's affair, as far as I had a knowledge of them, I had made it much fuller than the occasion demanded; I further asked a few questions in the belief that I would be allowed to have some interest in the matter as the uncle & guardian of the minor & on account of the peculiar ties wh bind him to me. Your letter, however, is silent on every point. Interested

I am deeply and under that feeling I wrote, but not to thrust myself illegally into the office of administrator.

I am sorry to see that the chief points of my letter have been misunderstood, as an additional delay will now occur, & the minor subjects I touched upon on a previous occasion will be needless; I will very briefly recapitulate the principal ones which will be sufficient.

Monk's Indian transactions were finally settled before he left Deyrah and Landour. I was betrayed, by my dread of not being able to meet the demand, into asking for the £130. I have since seen I could not ask the amount of you. All the deeds executed and transactions enterred [sic] into and completed, were previous to the 4th Dec—Monk's death occurred on the 9th and upwards of a hundred miles from the places he had left for ever. The documents which closed my transactions with Monk cannot concern the estate, and in showing them to the authorities here and to Mrs. Monk, and satisfying both, I have done all that can be desired of me.

Mrs. Monk administers to the estate of her husband and has begged me to act for her. She has constituted me her attorney and agent in all matters. I enclose a copy of the power. Much expense will be saved if you will lend your assistance and, as Monk's agent during his lifetime let me know the extent and nature of his property in Europe. In what manner his French funds were invested, and what is the amount of the remainder of the property and how disposed. Pray let all information be as explicit and official as possible, so that final arrangements may at once be made. I need not point out the benefit to the estate, which your cordial co-operation will bring. The taking out letters of administration and appointing an attorney in England will be very expensive and I would like, if possible, to avoid it. Any information you can give me regarding the understood wishes of Monk will be acceptable.

In the last place I must assure you that my advice will always tend to benefit Hugh, prevent the property being frittered away in disputes and unnecessary expences, ensure a provision for the widow and generally bring about an amicable settlement, so that none interested may have to complain.

Hugh sends his love to you, his aunt and cousins, and I trust he will be able very soon to introduce himself to his aunt thro' a letter written by himself in his best round hand.

Yours sincerely,
I. R. Lewin.

C41 of Register:
M. Fitzhugh Monk died Decr 9th, buried Decr 9th 1849.
St. John's Church, Meerut.
J.B.D'Aquilar, Asst Chaplain.

LETTER LXXXVII

From Dr. SPENSER, 3 Salutary Mount, Exeter
To Dr. N. MAGRATH R.N., Guernsey
[On mourning paper]

3 JUNE 1851

My Dear Sir,

Yesterday a letter from you addressed to me at Meerutt in March 1850 reached me through my agents.

The delay has been caused by my leaving India in the Feby of 1850 and you will at once see that it is not my fault that you did not receive from me all the particulars regarding the death of Mr. Monk which I could have furnished—had I been at Meerutt on the arrival of your letter—I should willingly have responded to your request. It is now I imagine too late for my information scanty as it is, to be of any service but I may as well state the little I remember.

Mr. Monk was unknown to me except by name when in the afternoon of, I think, the 8th of Decr 1849 he came to my house labouring under what appeared to me to be a serious attack of croup. His breathing was very laborious, and attending with a ringing noise in the windpipe. I sent him to the house where he was staying and followed directly myself—abstracted a large quantity of blood from his arm—applied hot fomentations to his throat & as soon as they could be procured a number of leeches were applied; these remedies appeared to afford some considerable relief and he became more composed and disposed to sleep—he had some medicine prescribed for him & I left him at night with orders that I should be sent for if any unfavourable change occurred.

I heard nothing from him during the night and when I called early in the morning, I was told that he had died, at what hour I now forget. Further enquiries elicited that he had suffered from difficulty of breathing for some time before, at least so it was said, that the attack from which he died, had come on while he was journeying from Landour to Meerutt.

I believe I expressed an opinion at the time, that, as death had ensued without strugling [?] after the difficult respiration had eased for some hours (therefore not from suffocation) and as the corpse was particularly pale. There might have been an aneurism of one of the larger arteries near the heart and the train of symptoms with this result were the consequence of the aneurism having burst but I was not permitted to verify the fact by a post mortem examination. Mrs. Monk was with her husband and seemed in great distress.

A certificate of his death will not, I presume be now necessary—I can only in conclusion regret that I had not the opportunity of aiding your enquiries at the proper time but should you think of any circumstances on which you imagine I may be able to enlighten you pray do not hesitate to write to me to the above address. I believe, however, that I have mentioned all that I know.

I left Meerutt in Jany 1850 and retired from the service in Feby. I remain my dear sir, yours faithfully, ... [?] ... Spenser.

LETTER LXXXVIII

From The Revd ISAAC LEWIN, Landour Academy
To NICHOLAS MAGRATH.

28 JULY 1851

My Dear Sir,

I have much pleasure in enclosing the required certificate of burial. Mrs. Monk has not taken out letters of administration, as under the circumstances, it would have entailed useless expense.

I have merely again to repeat my former request and express a hope that all matters may be amicably settled. Anything apart from this will only injure poor Hugh. I cannot conceive why my endeavour in the matter should be looked upon with suspicion. If you expect dishonesty, I fear you will be altogether disappointed. Pardon me for writing so openly. We are too far from each other to afford to lose time in not expressing ourselves openly. I may have omitted legal forms, but this has been from ignorance and a full persuasion that no difficulties would have been created to prevent the settlement of affairs.

Hugh is quite well and sends his love. Excuse my writing so concisely. I have had sickness in my family and lost my only child, so that I cannot immediately[?] fix my mind to a subject.

Yours sincerely,
I.R. Lewin.

LETTER LXXXIX

Copies of two MARRIAGE CERTIFICATES.

A. 9 August 1849. Mauger Fitz Hugh Monk of Full Age Widower Schoolmaster of Landour, son of Hugh Monk, by licence, to Ann Weller aged 15 Spinster of Landour, daughter of John Weller; by M. J. Jennings, Chaplain. Witnesses: Wm. Richard Ford, Herbert Grant Scott, Catherine Lewin, I. R. Lewin.

B. At Landour 10 June 1851 W. H. Johnson aged 19, Batchelor Surveyor of Landour, son of Thomas Johnson, by licence, to Ann Monk aged 16, Widow of Landour, daughter of John Weller by M. J. Jennings, Chaplain. Witnesses: W. R. Ford, I. R. Lewin, Hannah Lewin.

LETTER XC

From W. H. JOHNSON, Survey of India, Deyrah Dhoon
To NICHOLAS MAGRATH, St.Peter Port.

18 AUGUST 1851

Johnson, as husband of Mauger Monk's widow, says he has written to the Administrator General at Calcutta to question I.R. Lewin's and B.W. Lewin's conjoint taking possession of the property & documents of the late Mauger Monk "without sufficient authority". Ditto re the guardianship of Monk's son. Concern about a life annuity. But his chief object is to ask about Monk's French rentes & to declare his wife's entitlement, as Monk's widow, to one third of Monk's property, both in England & India. He asks for all necessary information and encloses copies of the two marriage certificates.

LETTER XCI

From W [?]. S. LACY, Asst Surgeon, in Medl
Charge of Mussoorie, Himalayah
To Dr. MAGRATH, Guernsey.

14 FEBRUARY 1854

My Dear Magrath,

My note of 3[?] mentioned having written to Mr. Johnston requesting him to come up to me, the old gentm came, he was formerly a conductor, now on the invalid estabt, a very respectable old man. His son who married Mrs. Monk is in the survey departt an assistt of some kind, I fancy, and is now with the head quarters of that departt at Attock on the Indus, having left his wife with her father at Deyrah. From the latter I got but little information, his daughter in law appears to have been a perfect child when left as a widow, and seems to have known little or nothing of the affairs or papers of her late husband, not even whether there was a will tho' from all accounts there appears to have been one, each party suspecting the other of having made away with it. Before calling on the Lewins I made as many enquiries as I could—the general impression is against them—how they shd have possession of the property when it is well known that they had not a farthing is a mystery to people. I called, and having made known the purpose of my visit to Mr. Lewin, asked whether he was willing to give all the information required—his answer was "certainly", and this is the sense and substance of what I learnt.

It appears that your poor brother-in-law (with whom I was at college) borrowed from the bank 12,000 Rupees for which sum the bank made him insure his life, besides taking the house in mortgage. On his wishing to go home (and to enable him to do so) Mr. Lewin agreed with Monk to take all his debts amounting to Rs 17,000 (the bank debt included) on himself—in consideration of Monk making over his property at Landour and a house at Deyrah (which property was valued at 12,000 Rs) to Mr. Lewin. Monk at the same time promised to remit from home the sum above, Rs 12,000. According to Mr. L no bond of any kind was given, but when Monk left Landour he said he would make out all necessary papers and send them up to Mr. L—his death at Meerut preventing this. Mr.Lewin went to Meerut to attend the funeral and says that no papers of any consequence were forthcoming! The title deeds or deed of sale transferring the houses to Mr. Lewin I carefully examined, they are made out on stamped paper and are duly witnessed. One of the witnesses who I hear was an intimate friend of your brother's will be here in about a month or six weeks, and from him I shall make all the enquiries. On the death of yr brother-in-law, the bank paid themselves from the policy, by this relieving Mr. L of that portion of the debt, who acknowledging that a 1/3 was due to the widow gave her a promissory note for Rs 4,000, which she (then Mrs. Johnston) finding there was little chance of his ever paying compromissed [sic] with him for 1000 Rs, which was paid and Mr. Lewin owns to owing the young boy 2/3 or Rs 8,000, but as there are no papers to prove that he is liable to that amount I imagine there would be no possibility of compelling him by law to make over the property in the child's name to cover that liability.

I saw the boy, he is a fine sprightly lad rather dark (the Lewins who are of Jewish extraction are themselves dark) I could trace no resemblance to his poor father, tho' the Lewins say there is a strong likeness. Mr. L told me that he was a sharp, clever boy, and from what I could learn from themselves, they appear to be fond of him. Mr. Lewin shewed me a paper signed by your brother, in which he constitutes Mr. L the lad's guardian, but it is no legal document. On my enquiring their intentions they (the old father, or as he introduced himself to me "old Lewin" was present) said they had no intention of parting with him but hoped to complete his education in England (this without assistance there is no chance I fancy of their being able to do). I will still make enquiries and shd I hear anything will let you know. If possible I will go down to Deyrah and question Mrs. Johnston, who having two young children was unable to accompany her father in law. I dare say it will sound strange but we have now got snow thick on the ground and icicles the length of my arm hanging from the eaves. I am in hopes to be able to remain up here until next October—the only thing which may prevent me is my promotion which I am very anxious not to get yet! Two months hence when the season commences I shall be in my saddle all day to say nothing of night work seven horses constantly at work. It is the hardest work appointment in all India! Two or three years hence D.V. you may see me again in old Guernsey (there are far worse places than it) as I am thinking of taking a furlough for a year about that time to bring home my two little boys.

Remember me very kindly to Carey who if memory serves faithfully is now your partner. Should you favour me again, pray give me some Guernsey news. I will be most happy to do all I can for you. Believe me,

Yours sincerely,
W [?]. S. Lacy.

LETTER XCII

From HANNAH TOUSSAINT, née LEWIN, Jullundur, Punjaub
To HUGH LEWIN MONK, 'Rotha' Wolvercote, Oxford.
[Extracts]

29 DECEMBER 1902

Your parents were married on the 26th Novr 1842 at Mussoorie by the Revd. R.P. Brooke. On the 26th Septr of the following year a daughter was born, who lived three days—she was baptised by the nurse & called Margaret. In '44 you came. On the 10th Septr 1846 another daughter was born at Hazelwood, Landour, & baptised Elizabeth Isabella. She died the following June, I have forgotten the date. Your mother's death on the 21st September 1846 caused me my first great sorrow, and nearly cost my father his life; for he fell in a dead faint on the pulelea [?] floor of the krauda [?]. Yet, we recovered the effects of the blow. We (he & my brother & I) were in Meerut at the time. She died at Hazelwood, Landour.

[Hannah is describing the skills of her father, B.L. Lewin & comparing them with those of Mauger.]

Your father was also very good—drawing and painting well taught, & he said, "Well Guv'nor', I could do nothing like that". All the same he didn't like guv'nor and guv'nor didn't like him. They were always arguing and what enraged the old man.

Monk never lost his temper. He was very good-tempered, a polished scholar, wonderful classic, spoke Parisian French, and beautiful Saxon English. But like so many others he overlooked what he excelled in and imagined he was a proficient in what he knew nothing about. He danced beautifully, and thought he could ride. He conversed charmingly, but fancied he could sing. Was very, very fond of the pleasures of the table—a gourmet, not a gourmand. In personal appearance he had a very nice tidy well-set figure, beautiful hands & small feet, always well chaussé—bien ganté, bien chaussé[?]. Not good-looking except for expressive brown eyes, plain in fact. Very grey as long as even I remember him.

Your mother was beautiful in every respect—character, mind and person. Brown eyes large and lustrous, a handsome nose like Dora's, good mouth, pretty chin & a forehead like a Madonna's. Pretty figure, too. She was like a mother to me, tho' only six years older. She instilled into me the love of good reading ... After your mother's death your father was wanting to marry every third girl he met—he didn't care who it was, he wanted a companion. Eventually as you know he married Annie Weller! A girl of 16 absolutely uneducated, but with a pretty face. Four months after he was taking her home, via the Cape, where he was intending to spend some time with his cousin Sir Harry Smith (husband of Ladysmith!). [Not a cousin. The Smith cousin was a different person. Ed.] He died at Meerut of quinsy Decr 1849. My brother went down, brought the young widow up & gave her a home till she married in '51, Wm. Johnson, Survey of India. You were left with me till he could arrange to send for you. You know the rest. He also left Mullingar with a debt of 17,000 Rs on it. "Monk and Lewin" Landour Academy had bought the house for 12,000 but Monk had mortgaged it in his own name & when your uncle volunteered to take the debt on himself Major Freeth the manager of the Mussoorie Bank tried to dissuade him from the "mad act". "You are hanging a millstone round your neck from which you will suffer till the end of your days" and he did.

Your father, like mine, left home after getting into some trouble (cherchez la femme), enlisted in the Royal [sic] Artillery under an assumed name, Fitzhugh O'Reilly, and came out to India. He was recognised by a friend of the family, Capt. Knatchbull, who wrote to old Dr. Monk that the prodigal had been discovered, his discharge was bought & now he had to earn his own living, for he refused to be taken into the bosom of the family again, tho' he accepted the forgiveness. He began teaching fencing, which his father disapproved of—"Be a dancing master at once"—then he answered Mr. Mackinnon's advertisement for a classics master. He came, & the principal thought to put him "through his paces". "Read me this passage in Virgil. I want to know how your quantities go." One glance at the passage & the book was put away and the passage & more were gone through from memory. John Mackinnon never forgave that triumph of his classical master! I don't think he remained long at that school. The next step, after he married was to buy a hotel! (They were all teachers in Mackinnon's school, my father writing master, brother under teacher). He (mis)managed the hotel for a year, was bankrupt and started a school. "Monk and Lewin". You were born during the period between winding up the hotel business and beginning of school. The hotel was at Rajpore on a magnificent scale—13 horses, 2 assistants, a veterinary surgeon, men servants and women servants. Four houses—an ice pit was started and I had the supervision of that, seeing it filled with snow from Mussoorie. The "Master" did all accounts and correspondence and book-keeping and Sedgeley, Cam & Co the attendance, drinking and fleecing. There was an amazing influx of visitors during that season. The "business" lasted not quite a year, not only in the spring when people went up to the hills & autumn when they went down, but all through the rains and summer.

The cuisine was unrivalled, the cards & billiards so attractive, "mine host" a gentleman, "such a great thing, you know". One "customer" I remember drank eleven cups of tea at a breakfast & the Khansama came, with tears in his eyes, to complain. The tea was the best "Howqua's Mixture" at I don't know how many rupees a lb. One autumn the money paid by people resting there on their way to the plains, used to be brought in daily in cheques and cash which could not be counted. (There were no currency notes then.) Everything was thrown into a drawer of which your mother was given the key. I helped to make a pretence of counting the rupees, & he gave "receipt in full", not knowing what was paid, nor how much pocketed by his establishment. I can't remember—I don't think I ever knew what happened to the business—the houses were a resort for some winters after & eventually someone bought the place I think—I don't know. After that Hazelwood & the Landour Academy which did not pay. My father, brother & I went to Meerut, also to teach. And on your mother's death returned to Landour & Mullingar was bought. I had you & the baby girl to comfort me; in June 1847 the little one died.

Your father, from time to time, used to tell us of his brothers & sisters & home in Guernsey. He was greatly attached to his sister Isabella (Bella) who was a regular correspondent of his. Of the boys' fun and naughtiness one incident stands out very prominently. I dare say I have often told you but it bears repeating. A neighbour of theirs in Guernsey, named Page, prided himself on a particular kind of geese, of which he had twelve, and a gander. William Monk the ringleader, Henry & Mauger one night stole the geese and tied a shilling piece to the gander's neck, with these words on the envelope that contained the coin:

"Pray Mr. Page don't be in a rage
But if you are we shan't wonder;
We've taken the geese at a penny a-piece
And left the cash with the gander."

LINES WRITTEN IN ISABELLA MONK'S HAND. NO DATE. NO AUTHOR STATED. APPLIES TO MAUGER MONK? ON BLACK-EDGED PAPER.

He left his home with a swelling sail
Of fame and fortune dreaming,
With a spirit as free as the vernal gale,
Or the pennon above him streaming.
He hath reached his goal; by a distant wave
'Neath a setting sun they've laid him;
And stranger forms bent o'er his grave,
When the last sad rites were paid him.

He should have died in his own loved land,
With friends and kinsmen near him;
Not have withered thus on a foreign strand,
With no thought, save of heaven, to cheer him.
But what recks it now? Is his sleep less sound
In the ports where the wild waves swept him,
Than if home's green turf his grave had bound,
Or the hearts he loved had wept him?
Then why repine? Can he feel the rays
That pestilent sun sheds o'er him;
Or share the grief that may cloud the days
Of the friends who now deplore him?
No—his bark's at anchor—its sails are furl'd
It hath 'scaped the storm's deep chiding;
And safe from the buffeting waves of the world,
In a haven of peace is riding.